Reviews

"Nancy LaPierre has done it again! As in her previous books, *Journey to a Better Land* and *God's Power Revealed Through Prayer*, she has woven spiritual lessons into the interesting stories she is telling. It was so easy for me when we had elderly parents living with us, to get so involved in caregiving that I would forget about what God was trying to teach me. Step by step, through the pages of *Courage for the Soul of the Caregiver,* Nancy helps us turn our face to God, so that we can receive His blessings. This book is going to be a great encouragement for caregivers who are caring for children, elderly parents, relatives, or other persons in need of care."

— *Pastor Richard Rose*

"This book is full of true-life experiences that offer encouragement and of examples of what God can do in every part of our lives. Reading from the caregiver's perspective is refreshing. The story flowed beautifully and is full of encouragement for all!"

— *Vicky Toliver, Elder and Caregiver*

"What a devotion and trust in God. A guidance on how to become a caregiver being devoted to the job at hand and trusting in God for guidance. The stories are so relatable and show Nancy being human but trusting in the scripture. You can read how over time she becomes stronger in faith and shows her special connection with her spirituality. I am not even close to Nancy's belief and trust in God. But her stories and guidance certainly show how truly glorious it can be."

— *Michaela M.*

Courage for the Soul of the Caregiver

Nancy Berthiaume LaPierre

TEACH Services, Inc.
PUBLISHING
www.TEACHServices.com • (800) 367-1844

All rights reserved. No part of this publication may be reproduced, distributed, or transmitted in any form or by any means, including photocopying, recording, or other electronic or mechanical methods, without the prior written permission of the publisher, except in the case of brief quotations embodied in critical reviews and certain other noncommercial uses permitted by copyright law. For permission requests, write to the publisher, TEACH Services, Inc., at the address below.

Copyright © 2020 Nancy Berthiaume LaPierre
Copyright © 2020 TEACH Services, Inc.
ISBN-13: 978-1-4796-1182-9 (Paperback)
ISBN-13: 978-1-4796-1388-5 (Hardback)
ISBN-13: 978-1-4796-1183-6 (ePub)
Library of Congress Control Number: 2020906887

All Scripture quotations, unless otherwise noted, are taken from the NEW KING JAMES VERSION (NKJV): Scripture taken from the NEW KING JAMES VERSION®. Copyright © 1982 by Thomas Nelson, Inc. Used by permission. All rights reserved.

Scriptures marked KJV are taken from the KING JAMES VERSION (KJV): KING JAMES VERSION, public domain.

All Scripture references followed by superscripts are found in the Scriptural Index.

Dedication

To all the caregivers in this world who sacrifice their time, energy, and lives to meet the needs of those around them.

Foreword

When I was caring for my mom, it became clearer every day what a challenge, what a responsibility, what a sacred trust, what a transforming experience this caregiving was. I found myself in an entirely new role. It was not like raising children, or being a wife, or working in a social setting. God had called me to serve Mom, and He promised to give me sufficient grace to do it. Slowly, but surely, my perceptions of this calling began to change. This book is about those changes, and it is written with the hope that my discoveries will encourage you. God bless your heart.

Preface

While caring for Mom for seven years, I made many discoveries that I would like to share with you about how to make every day a blessing. I know how challenging it is to care for a loved one—or for anyone who has been entrusted to you. In spite of the difficulties Mom and I faced daily, we loved each other. I wish with all my heart I would have laughed and shared more with her.

As you read my personal stories, may they help you to treasure every day with the precious soul(s) you are caring for. I pray that when you are finally separated from them you will have no regrets. I pray that you will have the hope of seeing them again when Jesus comes in the clouds.

The day is coming soon when Jesus will wipe all the tears from our eyes, and sickness, suffering, and death will be no more. Let us find comfort and courage in that loving promise.

As you read my personal stories, may they help you to treasure every day with the precious soul(s) you are caring for

Acknowledgments

The hands on the cover of this book belong to me and a dear Christian sister, Christa Thomas. I want to thank Christa for giving me the honor of photographing her hand with mine. The hands are a true representation of kindness, love, and compassion; they remind me of the many times Mom held my hand while growing up, guiding me into adulthood. I was very thankful that God gave me the opportunity to reverse the roles and to hold her hand, guiding her safely through the golden years.

I also want to dedicate the rose, that beautiful flower, to my mom. It was her favorite flower, and it is a symbol to me of how beautiful the souls are that we care for. Let us look past the thorns and prickliness of some of our charges and remember how all of us are wonderfully and fearfully made in His image. We are not to crush those fragile flowers, but shower them with God's love every day and watch them flourish.

I could not have completed this book that you now hold in your hands if it were not for a wonderful woman and editor named Charlotte. She helped me to make this book a real encouragement for all the caregivers out there. She truly was an immediate answer to my prayer when God sent her to me at just the right time. One of God's true angels. Thank you Charlotte!

Table of Contents

Mom, the Caregiver 15
God's Minutemen 17
My Grandmother, Our Caregiver 19
A Marriage Without God: Mom and Dad 21
Entering God's Service 23
Gifts from Above 25
A Changed Heart 27
Choices, A Caregiver's Worst Nightmare 29
Spiritual and Physical Healing 31
The Joy of Forgiveness 33
Being a Faithful Steward 35
Healing Through God's Law 37
The Tie that Binds 39
God's Earth Angels 41
Caring for Others 43
Utilizing Your Gifts 45
The Challenge 47
The True Meaning of Serving 49
Showing Christ's Love 51
Reaping the Results 53
Mom 56
The Stroke 58
The Hospital 60
Bringing Mom Home 62
Physical Therapy 64
Waiting for God's Answer 66

Life-Changing Decisions	68
Leaving Mom	70
Making Preparations	72
Mom Moves In	74
Learning to Trust	76
Combining Lives	78
God's Way	80
Disappointment	83
Clothed in God's Righteousness	85
Reaching the Goal	87
The Beautiful Light	89
Leaning on Jesus	91
God's Family	93
Brothers and Sisters in Christ	95
The Caregiver's Mission	97
Living in Harmony	99
Becoming Perfect Through Jesus	101
Dealing with Indecision	103
God's Watch Care over His Children	106
Blessing Others	108
Sharing the Good News—Jesus Is Coming Again!	110
The Death Sentence	112
Hope after Death	114
Getting a People Ready	116
A New Life	118
Inheriting the Earth and Living Forever!	120
Scriptural Index	122
References	125
About the Author	126

Mom, the Caregiver

Nevertheless I am continually with You;
You hold me by my right hand (Ps. 73:23).

The Berthiaume (BERTH-ume) home was bustling with excitement. Mémère (MEM-may) Larue, my grandmother, was coming to live with us, and we five kids could not wait for her arrival! She was my mother's mom, but we didn't know her very well because our family did not visit her too often. Mom loved her mother, but to go out and visit with five kids was not on the list of things to do. Much of our time was spent at home, so we also had little contact with most of our aunts and uncles. There were only four of them who really stayed in touch with us. They were the ones who kept Mom up to date on the family news.

As Mémère got on in years and could not take care of herself, she went to live with one of her sons. She stayed with his family for a bit, but the time came when it was not possible to be there anymore. So my mother took on the role of caregiver. I remember the excitement that filled the air the day when Mom announced Mémère was coming. Finally, we were going to get to know our Mémère! She spoke French which gave some of us the hope of possibly learning a bit of the language from her. Mom and Dad spoke it fluently, but they had not taught it to us.

> *You can trust the Bible to be true and, within its pages, you will find the encouragement, hope, and love that you need*

On the day Mémère arrived, we children stood watching at the window. It was raining hard, as the taxi stopped in front of our home. The door opened and a tiny woman stepped out holding an umbrella. When she stepped into our home, we children suddenly became quite shy. It was as if we were greeting a stranger. But as the days passed, we got to know who she really was, and we enjoyed our time together.

Sadly, soon after Mémère arrived, she had a stroke that affected her speech. She knew what she wanted to say, but her words often did not come out right. But instead of being angry or frustrated, she would make light of it, laughing at herself. This made us laugh with her, and we loved her for her sweet spirit. As the months went by, Mémère's health grew worse, which made Mom's workload heavy at times. It was hard on Mom. I watched her every day doing what she could, and sometimes I would catch her crying because things were so difficult. Mom was not a praying woman as far as I could see, and I don't think she knew the God of the Bible well, but I know that He was seeing all she was going through and He never left her side. Mémère eventually had another stroke, and this time she had to be placed in a nursing home, where she died soon after that.

> **Think about this:** Mom could have found so much comfort from reading God's Word. When you find yourself going through difficult circumstances, remember the God of the Bible is the same today as He was in days of old. He was there with His people while they endured all kinds of trials, and He promises to be there for you today. Psalm 73:23 says, "Nevertheless I am continually with You; You hold me by my right hand." You can trust the Bible to be true and, within its pages, you will find the encouragement, hope, and love that you need.

God's Minutemen

And the King will answer and say to them, 'Assuredly I say to you, inasmuch as you did it to one of the least of these My brethren, you did it to Me' (Matt. 25:40).

There were many times when I was young that Mom was a caregiver. Whenever someone needed help, Mom was there to lend a helping hand. One of those times I remember very well. It was a beautiful sunny day, and we children were playing, cleaning, and doing things that children do when they are home with Mom. That afternoon Mom answered a knock on the door and found our sweet Uncle David hunched over in pain and crying. He was in his twenty's, and had come home from college to visit his family. Mom helped him into the house while David kept saying over and over again that he thought he was going to die, begging her to help him. He was very pale, and Mom quickly assessed the situation and said, "Oh my, you must have a bad stomach virus." With the help of some of us, we managed to get him into Mom's bed and cover him up.

You don't have to be a trained caregiver to take up the tasks that God impresses you to do

Mom immediately became a caregiver to our uncle. She placed a cool cloth on his forehead and took his temperature. Then she started giving him liquids. Uncle David was in so much agony that he kept saying he thought he had been poisoned. He told us that he had eaten lunch out of a can that afternoon, and he thought the food was bad. We all tried to help him, but he was not getting better. In fact, things were getting worse, and Mom thought Uncle David just might die. Eventually she called an ambulance to take him to the hospital. We were all praying for Uncle David to get better.

We found out later that he had been poisoned. The doctors treated him, and, in a few days, he was better. We were so thankful for that because our Uncle David was the sweetest man, and God used him throughout his life. He was a Christian teacher for years, marrying my aunt Cathy Ann, who was also a wonderful Christian woman and teacher. Later Uncle David became a true minister of God, preaching in different churches. There were so many times that God saved my Uncle David from different things, including a few near-death experiences. He was a real man of God whom we all grew to love and trust. I am thankful that God sent him to my mom that day. She was calm and patient when it came to doctoring any of us, and it seemed that she always knew what to do.

> **Think about this:** God used my mom many times to take care of the ones who needed it. She never claimed to be a caregiver, but she was definitely a minuteman, ready at a moment's notice to help wherever she was needed. My Uncle David knew this, and, although other family members were nearby, he chose to come to my mom because he knew she would be there to help him—no matter how bad the situation was.
>
> You don't have to be a trained caregiver to take up the tasks that God impresses you to do. Mom may not have been a praying woman, but God knew just whom to appoint when someone was in need. When someone comes to you in need of a helping hand, remember that you, too, can become God's minuteman or minutewoman.

My Grandmother, Our Caregiver

*And it shall come to pass afterward that I will pour out
My Spirit on all flesh; your sons and your daughters shall
prophesy, your old men shall dream dreams, your young
men shall see visions. And also on My menservants and
on My maidservants I will pour out My Spirit in those days*
(Joel 2:28, 29).

As a young girl, I relied on my Dad's mom, my other grandmother, Mémère Berthiaume, to teach me what I needed to know about God. My grandmother knew how to be a wonderful caregiver to us children, knowing just what we needed. She was not only our caregiver, but also my mentor, and she taught me how to love. Whenever I had a problem, I would go to her for answers. She had a special relationship with God, and she would open her Bible asking Him for guidance. He never failed to give her the good counsel she was seeking.

I loved listening to my grandmother's stories. God became real to me as I listened to those precious stories of long ago. God used her to plant a strong faith in God in our family. We respected her because she was God's servant. He gave her a testimony for Jesus Christ, and she chose not to hide it, but to share it with everyone she knew.

Many people were blessed by my grandmother's words, but some of her own children rejected what she was teaching. My dad was one of them. I remember when she came to live with us for a while; she would see Dad smoking and drinking as he watched TV, and it broke her heart.

One night God gave her a dream. She shared it with me, explaining how Jesus was looking in the window of our apartment and watching our family. She explained that God had big tears in His eyes as He saw my dad making bad choices. She told Dad her dream, but it seemed to make him defensive, justifying his actions. But I shall never forget that dream.

Think about this: Mémère Berthiaume was God's messenger, bringing hope to people who needed to hear His word. We should respect what our God-fearing older folks have to say. They have more experience with life and are longing to tell their stories to benefit us.

As a caregiver to Grandmother Berthiaume, Mom never realized what a treasure she had staying with her. Both Mom and Dad rejected the counsel that God gave through Mémère, and eventually it resulted in a broken marriage. If they had only listened to her, they might have turned their marriage around.

As you are caring for the elderly, listen to what they have to say, for it might just be that God is trying to tell you something. People need to know Jesus as their Savior and Lord. Like my grandmother, Mémère Berthiaume, let us also be willing to be Christ's messengers, proclaiming to the world how He lived, died, and rose again to save us. Praise God!

A Marriage Without God: Mom and Dad

And the Lord God said, "It is not good that man should be alone; I will make him a helper comparable to him"
(Gen. 2:18).

In reflecting back, Mom and Dad met at a very young age; she was only fifteen and Dad was nineteen. They were attracted to each other right away and decided to date. Things were going well, and they were falling in love, but Mom was too young for a true commitment. Dad was a Christian man, always carrying his Bible everywhere he went. Then came the day that Dad decided to join the military for a few years. He had a burden to serve his country, and maybe—he reasoned, when his two-year commitment was up—Mom would be ready to marry him. While he was in the service, something happened. He didn't talk about God or carry his Bible anymore. Dad had become a changed man, drinking and smoking with the rest of his buddies. After serving his time, he returned home. Mom noticed the big change in him, but it did not seem to bother her. They were still in love, and, at the ages of seventeen and twenty-one, they were married by a justice of the peace. Her mom and dad were there, along with nine siblings, to help celebrate the happy occasion.

They waited two years before deciding to have a family, and then, to their delight, their first baby was born. Following this, my dad gave his heart to Jesus again. Then the babies kept coming, until there were five of us. Our home was a contented one with God at the center. Unfortunately, our happy family did not last. At his place of work, Dad made friends with those who were not a good influence. They encouraged him to start drinking and smoking again, and soon our home became an unloving place. There was verbal and physical abuse, and the marriage that once held such promise became a place of fear for all of us.

Our home was far from what it should have been, and Mom's feelings toward Dad were starting to change. She blamed him for the situation they were in. Parents are supposed to be the best caregivers, bringing up their children with love. Mom and Dad let go of their responsibility as parents, which would have been a complete disaster for us were it not for our godly grandmother. She was the one who held most of us together. Her love was strong.

> **Think about this:** Marriage is the union of two people standing together—sharing their joys, sufferings, and feelings. Two people becoming one flesh means being completely one in body, mind, and heart, yet remaining as two separate individuals. While they are still two people, a married couple is supposed to be working together as partners to make their home a safe and happy one. Dad never understood this, and we all suffered for it. Eventually my mom became my father's caregiver. It was difficult to watch her struggle with such a great responsibility.
>
> If you find yourself having to care for your spouse or anyone else—whether as the result of their wrong choices or because of some other reason—seek strength from God, and He will bless you.

Entering God's Service

Your word I have hidden in my heart, that I might not sin against You (Ps. 119:11).

Mom and Dad both gave their lives to Jesus early in their marriage. When they started their life together, Mom came to know and love God through my grandmother, Dad's mom. Mom understood what God required of her to become His child. They both had God's Word in their hearts, and they started their family. Those were happy times, going to church together and really having a loving home. As each baby arrived, it became more difficult to bring us all to church. Mom and Dad started to backslide and make bad choices. God's word did not stay in their hearts, and they broke their covenant relationship with Him. They no longer cared to do God's service.

Oftentimes, at the end of the week, Dad would not come home from work right away, and we knew he was in some barroom, drinking. He often spent his entire paycheck on drink, instead of bringing the money home to his family who really needed it. He did not drive a car for very long before his drinking caused accidents. Many times, my mom had to go to the police station to pick him up after he was arrested for either driving while intoxicated or picking a fight with someone at the bar.

Someone had to take responsibility for the younger children. That responsibility fell on my sister and me. We were forced to care for the rest of the household as best we could

Life was becoming progressively worse at home because of Dad's drinking. What a lot of caregiving needed to be done—but, because my mom was so hurt by all of this, she retreated into her own world, which never included us. Someone had to take responsibility for the younger children. That responsibility fell on my sister and me. Even though we were then only ten and twelve years old—just children ourselves—we were forced to care for the rest of the household as best we could.

> **Think about this:** You may someday find yourself having to care for another person, whether or not you possess the knowledge or grace that is needed. If the task of being a caregiver is dropped on you unexpectedly, how will you respond? Will you grumble and complain, thinking you can't do this? God will show you the way and supply all your needs. Remember, you are a child of the King, and you gave your life over to Him and His service. Keep in mind you are working for Jesus. Keep His Word in your heart always, and you will never break your covenant relationship with Him. He wants you to enter into that service with joy and with a thankful heart—no matter what you are asked to do. Ephesians 6:7 says, "…with goodwill doing service, as to the Lord, and not to men."

Gifts from Above

*Every good gift and every perfect gift is from above, and
comes down from the Father of lights, with whom there is
no variation or shadow of turning* (James 1:17).

I discovered my natural abilities at an early age, as my sister and I were thrown into the role of parenting our younger siblings. We struggled to think of ways to make the household better. Many times, I found myself being a caregiver to Mom as well as Dad. Whenever Dad had too much to drink and was in a rage at Mom for some reason, she would call me to come and try to calm him down. I became their peacemaker. My experience with my parents helped me become a caregiver in later life.

At a young age, I begged Mom to buy the ten-volume set of *The Bible Stories,* * which she eventually did. I remember taking my younger brother into a quiet room and reading to him from those books every day. I wanted to show him that there was a better way of life for all of us—something different from what we were seeing at home. After giving my heart to God, it seemed that I was given, through the Holy Spirit, the gift of mercy. This gift helped me in my role of caregiving, for which I am very thankful.

> **Think about this:** God gives His children spiritual gifts and ministries in order to bless others. These gifts are a witness to the world that God is love, and they are given to us by the Holy Spirit. In 1 Corinthians 12:11, it says, "But one and the same Spirit works all these things, distributing to each one individually as He wills." These gifts are not rewards, but they are the tools we need to perform the ministry He has called us to.
>
> To be a good caregiver, one must possess the gift of mercy to show others the love of God—Who is the source of all compassion and mercy. Don't neglect the gift that God has given you, but nourish it, and it will grow. Pray every day with the ones He

has given you to care for, showing kindness and mercy in all situations, making your time together as pleasant as possible. Think about the influence you can have for good when you have God's Spirit within you.

*Maxwell, Arthur S. *The Bible Story* (10 volumes). Washington, DC: Review and Herald Publishing Association, 1953–1957.

A Changed Heart

He who believes and is baptized will be saved; but he who does not believe will be condemned (Mark 16:16).

I made the decision at a young age to commit my life to Jesus, and, as a result, I was baptized at the age of thirteen, being fully immerged in water—as Jesus was when He was baptized by John the Baptist (John 3:23).[1] Growing up in an alcoholic, dysfunctional home, I chose not to follow in my parents' footsteps. I never would have guessed that the life God had planned for me would include the role of a caregiver. Mom had taken care of her mom, and her example impressed me to take on this selfless act of caring for the needs of others.

I started my caregiving within my own family long before my baptism, trying to keep us all together. This was not easy to do. Years later, I remembered when Mom tried to commit suicide because she was so miserable. On that day, she went out with my dad's brother, claiming she needed some groceries. I felt in my heart that she was leaving for another reason. I remember being so worried about her at that time. It was not even an hour later that she burst into the house screaming, and my uncle explained to us that, while he was driving, she had opened the car door and flung herself out into the street. For some unknown reason, he brought her straight home instead of taking her to the hospital. Her face was disfigured, and her entire body was badly hurt. My sisters and I had to take care of her as she recovered. Our younger sister bore the brunt of caring for our mother because my older sister and I were working at the time. That was a very tough time for all of us, but with God's help, we made it through. As I was growing older, I started doing more and more caregiving for other people, and I soon found out that I loved being a caregiver.

Think about this: When you decide to follow Jesus, you are called out of the world's ways of living, but then you are sent back into the world as Christ's servant and disciple, with a longing in your heart to serve and honor Him. A new life is waiting. Your old sinful ways are gone and you are alive now only to God (Rom. 6:3, 4).[2] Show others what Christ has done in your life by all your actions, and offer them the opportunity to come to love Him, too. You will not be perfect. Only through Jesus Christ can you carry on from day to day, learning the lessons He is trying to teach you. You may fall many times, but He will help you up saying, "Go on; I am here by your side always." Praise God! This is the hope you have because you are a child of the King!

Choices, A Caregiver's Worst Nightmare

I beseech you therefore, brethren, by the mercies of God, that you present your bodies a living sacrifice, holy, acceptable to God, which is your reasonable service. And do not be conformed to this world, but be transformed by the renewing of your mind, that you may prove what is that good and acceptable and perfect will of God
(Rom. 12:1, 2).

Christian behavior was not practiced in the home where I spent the first twenty years of my life. Not only were we exposed to Mom and Dad's wrong choices, but Uncle Sandy, Dad's brother, would come over, bringing lots of alcoholic beverages with him. Mom and he would spend quite a bit of time drinking, singing, and laughing together. Eventually Dad would get involved, and that was when the fighting would start. Their wrong choices caused their bodies to grow old quickly, eventually becoming diseased. Dad smoked for most of his life, and he eventually died of lung disease. Uncle Sandy had one-half of his foot amputated because of diabetes and the continual level of alcohol in his bloodstream. After my uncle's amputation, he continued to drink heavily, not learning from his mistakes. He eventually died of a heart attack, while he was drunk! His heart could not take all that alcohol any longer, and it finally gave out. He was only sixty-eight years old at the time.

What a shame that Dad and my uncle Sandy did not heed the warning signs that told them a change was needed. They were conformed to this world, enjoying all it had to offer. Unfortunately, their poor choices led to their destruction. My grandmother had taught them right from wrong. She had tried her best to warn them about their behavior, and she constantly prayed for her children, but they chose to go the world's way instead. God shows us the right path to follow, but we make our own choices. How different our home life would have been if they had only listened to what God was saying and lived a Christian lifestyle.

We are called by God to live a life that will not lead to self-destruction. When we make wise choices, as Jesus did, we experience the true joy our Heavenly Father wants for us. Consuming the world's pleasures causes people to think they are feeling good. They may experience that feeling for a little time, but eventually those pleasures destroy them.

> *We are called by God to live a life that will not lead to self-destruction*

I know from personal experience how alcohol destroys families. It was devastating to us five children and Mom to live with an alcoholic father. We lived in fear, and our own health suffered. We lost much rest and sleep, listening to the constant fighting, always wondering if we would be next to experience Dad's anger.

The smoking was just as bad. We were constantly exposed to secondhand smoke, and, as a result, we were often sick. It was terrible watching Dad slowly die, unable to breathe well. My dad and uncle broke the sixth commandment, "Thou shalt not kill" (Exod. 20:13, KJV), by killing their own bodies. God is so sad when he sees us doing these things to ourselves.

> **Think about this:** Caregivers witness the results of their patient's choices and actions. When it comes time for us to care for these souls, it can make us angry when we have to clean up the mess they made because of a lifetime of their own bad decisions. At times, this caregiving will not be easy, especially with the elderly, because they tend to be set in their ways. Often, like Dad, they deceive themselves into thinking that nothing they did in their lifetime was wrong. Nobody could convince him at the time that drinking alcohol was bad. He always claimed he had the body of a twenty year old and was going to live forever. Then, the time came when his once-young body fell apart from all his abuse. At that point, the only thing we could do was to gently care for him, pointing his thoughts toward heaven, so that he would ask for forgiveness and receive the peace of mind that only comes from God.

Spiritual and Physical Healing

*Or do you not know that your body is the temple of the Holy
Spirit who is in you, whom you have from God, and you
are not your own? For you were bought at a price; therefore
glorify God in your body and in your spirit, which are God's*
(1 Cor. 6:19, 20).

While my childhood home was always in a state of chaos, there was a place of refuge where I could spend some quiet, happy times. Dad's sister, my aunt Jeannette, and I got along quite well. She had two sons who were younger than I, and I would babysit them on occasion. My aunt had an addiction that was just as bad as my dad's—but not with alcohol. There is another addiction that can be just as deadly: drug abuse. My aunt often experienced a great deal of pain, and she had been prescribed several pain drugs. I was unaware of this addiction. We would sing and laugh for hours, and I never realized that she was destroying her body with the misuse of those drugs.

As she became older, her body grew increasingly tolerant of larger doses of pain drugs until none of the pills would work. In addition, her immune system was starting to break down. Eventually her son, Emile, had to become her caregiver. At times, it was devastating for him, but he did a wonderful job. Caregiving is emotionally difficult and draining, as you watch your loved one suffer, knowing you can't change the situation, but can only care for the victim. My aunt had brought most of those health issues on herself. She did not heed the counsel that was given her concerning her medications. Trusting more in God for the spiritual healing she needed would have contributed greatly to her physical healing.

> **Think about this:** Let us honor God by living as Jesus did. He is our example of Christian living. All true obedience comes from the heart. Christ was completely surrendered to His Father's will

for Him. When we surrender to God. as Christ did, He gives us the power to do His will. We will want to take care of our bodies, knowing we are not our own, that He has ransomed us with His blood. When we look upon the crucified Savior, realizing everything He has done for us, we will want to please Him. Our thoughts will no longer be on ourselves and the things of this world. The apostle Paul says, "…just as I also please all men in all things, not seeking my own profit, but the profit of many, that they may be saved (1 Cor. 10:33).

Show the ones you care for that there is a better way—that all they have to do is go to Jesus and surrender their lives into His keeping. Soon their minds and bodies will be feeling much better. Christ came to this earth "…that they may have life, and that they may have it more abundantly" (John 10:10).

In 1 John 2:6, it says, "He who says he abides in Him ought himself also to walk just as He walked." Let us give God control of this wonderful body that He has blessed us with, so that we can praise and glorify Him in it!

The Joy of Forgiveness

*Blessed is he whose transgression is forgiven, whose sin is
covered. Blessed is the man to whom the Lord does not
impute iniquity, and in whose spirit there is no guile*
(Ps. 32:1–2).

Dad's mom, my grandmother, gave her heart to Jesus when she was very young. Several of her aunts were nuns, and they impressed her to follow in their footsteps. They invited her to live with them at the convent, and, at the age of 10, she went. After a few years, she returned home. However, becoming a nun continued to consume her thoughts, and she decided to go and live at another convent. A total of ten years passed with her trying to do what she thought God wanted her to do. The day finally came when she understood that she was not really called to be a nun. Instead, her mind became filled with thoughts of getting married someday and raising lots of children for the Lord. She decided it would be best to study God's word for herself. Her mom owned a Bible, and the two of them started studying it together, learning many new truths.

One day, at the age of twenty-one she met a very handsome young man and fell deeply in love. The two married and started a beautiful life together with God at the center. During the course of those years, their family grew to include six children, fulfilling the promise to raise lots of children for the Lord! Unfortunately, my grandfather started drinking heavily, and this caused my grandmother to become very discouraged. Their marriage was not going well. One day, at the age of fifty-eight, my grandfather went to my grandmother and asked for her forgiveness, saying how sorry he was for the sadness he had brought to their home and expressing his undying love for her. Not long afterward, he died, the awful bottle by his side.

Learning to forgive was very difficult for me. Some of Mémère's children, including my dad and his brother, took the wrong path in life and followed in my grandfather's drinking ways. Growing up in our dysfunctional home, exposed to alcohol, smoking, and verbal and physical abuse, was very hard. I not only had to forgive my parents, but I felt that my uncle had also played a big part in the disruption of our lives. It seemed he was always there, laughing and having a good time with Mom, while they drank together. Mom was not a heavy drinker, but she did not discourage the activity. Dad would come home from work to find them both in this condition. He would be very jealous.

Dad did most of his drinking alone, and he was not as happy-go-lucky of a drinker as my uncle was. Dad would drink until anger consumed him. There was a lot of selfishness and wrong choices in our family. My parents tried to find their way using the bottle, but it was not working—it never does. And we five children were caught in the middle. We needed someone; fortunately, we had my grandmother who cared for us and showed us the true Caregiver who sees all that is going on. She taught us about a loving Savior who died for our sins. Through her, we learned that there was a better, happier way to live. We could see by observing our parents how their choices affected our whole lives and the lives of those around us. God was watching over us, and we grew up determined to not make the same mistakes. It was very hard for me to forgive my parents, and I had to really pray that God would give me a heart to do it. I loved my parents and wanted them to be a part of my life. God was showing me through studying the Bible and through His people how to forgive them. I could not feel the true joy of serving my Savior until the hatred that was harbored in my heart like a cancer was removed.

> **Think about this:** Christ is our greatest example of caregiving, full of love and compassion toward us who are sinners. If you find yourself caring for those who are in need of healing, pray that God will enable you to guide them in the right direction. Tell them that there is a God in Heaven who cares and is ever ready to make intercession for them. Take the time to go to Him and rest in His love for you. Share your needs; unburden your heart. We are told to come "boldly to the throne of God" (Heb. 4:16).[3] God is more than willing to give you strength and show you the way. Put your trust in Him as you work.

Being a Faithful Steward

Let a man so consider us, as servants of Christ and stewards of the mysteries of God. Moreover it is required in stewards that one be found faithful
(1 Cor. 4:1, 2).

Another opportunity presented itself for me to practice my caregiving abilities when I was in my teens. My aunt, my mom's sister, was very sick and dying of a liver disease at the young age of 32. What a sad time! She needed someone to help her at home for a while, so Mom decided to send me. I was excited to be able to help her. I remember my uncle coming to pick me up, and we started on our way. When we arrived, my aunt seemed in good-enough spirits. The work was not hard, and the days went by quickly. It was not very long before it was almost time to go back home.

One evening, while my aunt and I were talking at the table, she told me stories about my sister and me when we were young. I enjoyed her stories, until she apologized to me for not having loved me as much as she loved my sister. This hurt me very much. I hadn't known she favored my sister over me then, even though I was the one who was helping her now. I had to give it all to God and try my best to continue to have a happy outlook on things. I knew she was not ungrateful, as some people can be. She did tell me how happy she was that I was able to come and take care of her when everyone else was too busy. My aunt died shortly after that incident, and I never regretted the time that I gave her.

Think about this: Living a Christian life means surrendering all, including yourself, unconditionally. The Scripture clearly states that everything belongs to God (Ps. 24:1).[4] Christ gave up everything so that we could be saved. This instills in us a longing to give something back to Him. Knowing what Jesus has done for us, we no longer want to live selfishly; instead, we want to do everything we can to make Him happy.

We become God's faithful stewards by using our abilities and time wisely and unselfishly. By so doing, we glorify Him and will be rewarded for it. Colossians 3:23, 24 says, "And whatever you do, do it heartily, as to the Lord and not to men, knowing that from the Lord you will receive the reward of the inheritance; for you serve the Lord Christ."

God will give you many opportunities to be a faithful steward for Him. Use your time and abilities to show Jesus to others, and always give your best to whatever task you find yourself doing. Remember, you will be rewarded; maybe not in this lifetime, but surely when Jesus comes to take you home.

Healing Through God's Law

Therefore the law is holy, and the commandment holy and just and good (Romans 7:12).

When I was a young woman of twenty, my brother invited me to accompany him to some Bible studies he was attending. This was his attempt to help me forget my troubles, since I had just broken up with my boyfriend of four years, and that was devastating. He decided that he would become my caregiver. He thought that meeting new friends and having a chance to get out of the house would be great for me. Living in an abusive home with Mom and Dad did not show me how to live the way I should. God knew I needed to get out of that environment to heal completely.

I was young, and I really needed the companionship of people my own age. The Bible studies proved to be wonderful. There were not a lot of us, but the fellowship was perfect. We talked many times about Jesus and His love. My healing began as we studied God's law and touched on the points that were so necessary for me to hear. I already had given myself to Him at the age of thirteen, but the love for my ex-boyfriend was robbing me of what God really wanted for me. God led me to those studies, and I learned, once again, what Jesus did for me. It is beholding Jesus that changes us through the power of the Holy Spirit. I thank Him for His love and for His law that shows me how to live completely in His will. I was learning that a successful relationship could not be established if I was not right with God. I needed to be seeking first His kingdom and His righteousness.

When I went to the Bible studies, I was shown a respect I was not accustomed to. The young people in the Bible study group genuinely cared about me. Through their actions, they showed me Jesus's love, reminding me that I was God's child. I was finally feeling a sense of belonging again, not only to this group, but to my Heavenly Father. They loved me unconditionally, no matter what my background was. My brother faithfully took me every week to fellowship with them, and I was learning more and more of what God had in store for me.

> **Think about this:** There are different kinds of caregiving in this world. God sent those wonderful friends who took care of me when I needed healing. He chose just the right ones who would be of help. God wants us to have that kind of unselfish love for others. John 13:34 says, "A new commandment I give to you, that you love one another; as I have loved you, that you also love one another." This commandment was not to replace the Ten Commandments, but it was to reveal—through Christ's example—what truly unselfish love really is. The first four Commandments teach us how to love the Lord our God with all of our heart, mind, and strength, and the last six Commandments teach us how to love our neighbor as ourselves. Whatever the role of caregiving God gives to you, always try to do your best. He will never fail you or the ones you are helping.
>
> We would do well to follow and obey God's Law because obedience shows love and respect. Christ obeyed the Law to the fullest in His life. As believers, we recognize how Christ always valued the Law. There are many blessings that come from obedience, and, when we obey, the desire to live like Him grows in our hearts. Then, as caregivers, we will be able to show the love and compassion we would want shown to us if we were in need. At the cross, Christ set us free from the curse and penalty of sin. Delight to do God's will and place His law in your heart, as the psalmist David did, and then God's love will flow through you to everyone you come in contact with.

The Tie that Binds

Husbands love your wives, just as Christ also loved the church and gave Himself for her (Eph. 5:25).

As I was growing older, the determination not to make the same mistakes as my parents had made grew strong within me. I chose whom I would date wisely, staying away from the smokers and drinkers. While I was attending the Bible studies, I met a nice guy named Mark who loved God and wanted to learn more about Jesus. He was the same age as I was and seemed to be everything I wanted in a lifelong mate. As we studied God's word together, I was happy to discover what a real relationship was all about, one that had true love in it. This was the kind of love God wanted me to have. The day before our marriage, Mark was baptized, truly believing God and everything God wanted for him. He was such a caring man, which showed me from the start that I was going to have a different life from what I had experienced in my parents' home. God would be the foundation and center of our family. We were married and became one, with Christ as the Head of our home.

As a caregiver to my children, I realized that my love had to be sacrificial and unconditional

What a difference it made to live in a Christian environment! We had worship every morning and every night. God gave us three beautiful boys to bring up for Him. Mark took on his role as husband and father to the best of his ability. Things were not always perfect, but our hearts were in the right place. We constantly prayed for God's guidance and direction. As a new mom, I had to learn what God expected of me, something I had never learned while living at home with my parents. God was still showing me every day how to live a Christian life through my husband and children.

As I was raising my family, God was teaching me that I was special and His partner. He taught me that I was responsible for the shaping and training of the characters of my children. It was not easy to do this tremendous job that was placed before me, but, with God's help, I was determined to give it my all. Nurturing my three sons was a new kind of caregiving for me. As a caregiver to my children, I realized that my love had to be sacrificial and unconditional. They needed to feel safe and respected. Children who feel unloved try to gain attention and express their anger through undesirable behavior. Those who feel secure and know that their parents love them will not only be happy to receive good gifts, but will also be willing to give of themselves. They will grow up to be healthy and happy.

> **Think about this:** God gave us marriage and a husband and family to care for, and He wants us to be a loving spouse and parent. This is the biggest caregiving job you will ever have, whether or not you have children. It is just as important to nurture and take care of your spouse. Pray often for the wisdom that is needed and learn to rely on Him. Even with all of this, the road will not be easy. Sometimes you may feel like a failure, but be assured God is with you. He watched over and protected me and my siblings when Mom and Dad didn't. If we allow Him, He will be the strong tie that binds us together, and He will not fail us.

God's Earth Angels

Therefore, whatever you want men to do to you, do also to them, for this is the Law and the Prophets (Matt. 7:12).

It was January 13, a cloudy and misty day. We were living in a school bus at the time—a place that we chose to live in while we paid to put our children through Christian schools. It was more affordable than living anywhere else. We lived on top of a mountain in New Hampshire. Two of my three children were attending the small Christian school that was located about twenty minutes away from us. This particular morning was very dreary, and my children woke up not feeling well, especially my oldest, Aaron. I was thinking of keeping us all home, but Mark had told me before he left for work that I should go to town and get some strong tape that we really needed. We always put this around the hose on the outside of the bus, to keep it from freezing and breaking. We had hooked up the hose to some friends' water spigot, so we could have water in the warmer weather. I decided to go to town, so I loaded my laundry into the car to wash at the laundromat near the school. I made some hot soup to take along with us for the boys' lunches. It would warm them on a chilly day. I knew it was raining, but it did not seem to be as cold as it had been in the recent past. Maybe it was thirty degrees that morning compared to ten degrees the day before.

I bundled up three-year-old Andrew and made sure eight-year-old Tim and ten-year-old Aaron were dressed for the cold. We had our morning worship and prayer, and it was now time to go. We got into our small car and started on our way. We had to go down a steep hill to get to the road that led to town. The road looked wet and black, but that was not out of the ordinary. I had no idea that the road was covered with black ice! The temperature had been at freezing the night before, and, with the warmer temperature and mistiness that morning, it just made the road look glazed. We started down the hill, when suddenly the car started to swerve and slide. I panicked! There was another car coming toward us from the other direction and we collided. My car flew into a snowbank, which thankfully stopped us, but not without totaling the car. The other car also flew into a snowbank, but the driver, passengers, and their vehicle were okay.

It was only minutes before I heard the sounds of an ambulance and police car. But they, too, slid off the road and into the snowbanks. My neck was hurting, and I found out that I had whiplash. Tim was sitting beside me, and he seemed alright, but later we learned that he had a concussion. Aaron had a broken leg, and little Andrew was knocked unconscious. As I looked around, I could not believe this was all happening. I had never had an accident before this.

We were taken to the hospital. I stayed with Aaron and Andrew because of their serious injuries, while my husband stayed with Tim, who was less seriously injured. While we were in the hospital, I met another mother who had just lost her husband and now faced losing her little boy as well. My heart went out to her! I knew my son would be coming home, but that sweet mom did not have much to look forward to. The extent of caregiving that I saw being given to us by those nurses while in that hospital was amazing. They not only cared for the children, but for us moms as well.

When it was finally time to leave, we did not want to go back to the bus. My children still needed extra care, but I did not know what to do. Then a wonderful church member offered her home to us while we recovered. I will never forget those nurses and the church member who showed such Christian love to us at the time. We all recovered and praised God for the wonderful caregivers that He had placed in our path. They were truly God's earth angels.

Think about this: Whether you are a nurse or some other kind of caregiver, always remember to place yourself in your patient's shoes. Sometimes this is hard, especially for those who are working in a hospital. Nurses—like others who work in stressful situations each day—can become very tired and may not exhibit the love they should be showing. It took a lot of love for the nurses that we met at the time to deal with my children as well as with other patients in the ward. My son was really rambunctious, and another little boy, as sick as he was, seemed to fall right into the same path as my son. They surely gave those nurses a time!

Treat others as you would want to be treated if the situation was reversed. Remember the golden rule found in this section's Scripture.

Caring for Others

The Lord watches over the strangers; He relieves the fatherless and widow.... (Psalms 146:9).

My mind often wanders back over those years when Mom took care of different people who needed her. I sometimes think *what a selfless act to do for another human being.* Mom saw a need and she filled it. She surely had the gift of mercy. By watching her, I learned that taking care of the sick was not easy. It takes a lot of patience, kindness, and selfless love; and I felt a growing desire inside of me to do the same someday.

Later, after having made the decision to educate our children in Christian schools, I began looking for jobs that would allow me to work around their school schedule so I could always be there for them when they came home. I cleaned houses and our church for much-needed pay. I also helped people in their homes, especially the elderly. I charged very little and sometimes nothing at all for those jobs. My reward was seeing their happy, grateful faces. It always put a smile on my own face, and God always blessed my efforts.

I can recall many fond memories of helping the elderly. My heart was warmed when they would say how much they appreciated the kindness shown to them. Until we put ourselves in their place, we can never understand what it means to have someone come in, do a load of laundry, wash the dishes, or just check to see if they are okay. At that time, the elderly I served were from a different generation than I was. Some of them did not care for the modern conveniences I enjoyed. They often ignored the dishwasher and refused to use a microwave. They didn't think the floor was clean unless it was scrubbed on one's hands and knees. Although I did not agree, I still loved listening to their stories of times past as I worked.

However, there were a few who were ungrateful and grumpy. It seemed that no matter what I did for them, they were never happy. These were the ones who needed mercy and compassion the most. I had to try to put myself in their place and feel their frustrations. My ministry was to make life easier for everyone, showing Jesus at all times. Praying and encouraging them helped a lot. I always asked myself, "What would Jesus do?" Then He would give me the answer I needed at the time, and the outcome would always be better.

> **Think about this:** My work took me to many who needed my help, including strangers. God is not a respecter of persons (Acts 10:34, KJV). You don't have to be acquainted with someone personally to respond to his or her needs. As Psalm 146:9 says, "The Lord watches over the strangers; He relieves the fatherless and widow." When God sent people into my path and impressed me to go and care for them, it didn't matter who they were. This is the greatest witness to God's children—that we care for them in their time of need, letting them know that Jesus loves and cares for them. Working with God gives you the opportunity to open His Word to those who are suffering, giving them hope.

Utilizing Your Gifts

As each one has received a gift, minister it to one another, as good stewards of the manifold grace of God (1 Peter 4:10).

Every day God was showing me more of the gifts He had given me. I not only had the gift of mercy, like Mom, but also the gift of hospitality, which gave me great joy! I was given the chance to fully utilize both of these gifts while I was married—especially when we lived in Maine. After living in the bus for six years in New Hampshire, we decided that we really needed to make a move for the children's sake. We still believed in Christian education, but we wanted to be near a school that had more than eight grades, so we could keep our children living at home with us for a little longer rather than sending them to a Christian boarding school. God led us to Norridgewock, Maine, where there was a wonderful Christian school that met all of our criteria. We lived in that town for sixteen years, and that is where I was able to use my God-given gifts and abilities to the fullest, as I was heavily involved with our church and neighbors.

Every week after church, we held a big potluck at our home. We would invite visitors from the church because some of them had come from afar, and they needed a place of fellowship, just to rest for a while and definitely to eat, before heading out again. Church members were also welcomed, and even our neighbors would come and join us. It was a wonderful time to share together and to be a witness for our faith. There were so many who needed prayer and encouragement for whatever their situation was at that time. It was truly a place of solace, where everyone felt loved. Our doors were always wide open for anyone who needed a helping hand or just needed someone to talk to. I thank God for using us to minister to others, for it was such a blessing to us as well!

Think about this: As a believer in Christ, we need to be able to witness about our faith, telling others what God has done for us. The purpose of spiritual gifts is to enable us to share our witness successfully with others. Just as the apostles prayed for power to witness and lead souls to Jesus, we should be praying also. We need to pray daily for the baptism of the Holy Spirit, confessing and repenting of our sins. By studying the Scriptures every day, the Holy Spirit will impress our minds with what our gifts are. These gifts will give us great joy, and other people will recognize them as well. It is also important to understand that we have all been given at least one gift to use in His service.

Thank God for spiritual gifts! What a blessing to be able to work for Him, ministering with those gifts He has given to us through the Holy Spirit. Let us not refuse them, for then we will be as accountable as the unfaithful servant who hid his talent in the ground until his master came back. Jesus explained the consequences of that action. He longs to share these gifts with you, not for you to hide them under a bushel, but so that you can utilize them for His glory (Matthew 25:24, 26–30).[5]

The Challenge

Go therefore and make disciples of all the nations, baptizing them in the name of the Father and of the Son and of the Holy Spirit (Matt. 28:19).

As my children grew older and started to reach the teen years, they became more independent. I was often on my knees seeking guidance and strength to know how to handle each situation, trying to let go and let God lead. This was very hard for me. As a mom, I wanted them to grow up loving the Lord and not make some of the same mistakes I had. I really had to come to realize that they were their own persons, and they had to live their own lives. My job was to teach them right from wrong, show them God's love, and then let Him take over.

Then came the day that God gave us seven more children to care for, in addition to our three. Upon learning that a Christian academy in Freeport, Maine, was looking for dorm parents for the boys' dormitory, we decided to interview for the job. Everything went very well, and they hired us! Oh my! Talk about a challenge! If we thought that raising three boys was difficult, we had no idea what was in store for us!

During that school year, there were a lot of ups and downs with the boys. This was truly caregiving in a different sort of way. We had to show unbiased love to each child. It was not an easy task to make all the right decisions as each problem arose. Unlike their own parents, these boys were not used to us, and the first thing we had to do was to gain their trust. Some were far from home and desperately needed a Mom and Dad. Mark and I surely needed God's help in order to be patient, kind, and forgiving. I felt that we were given this job by God, so that He could teach us how to be better parents—not only to our three children but also to all of these boys—bringing all His children closer to Him by our actions and helping them become His disciples.

I know God was involved in what we were doing. He was not distant or detached from us, but was very interested in everything that went on in our lives. God teaches in His Holy Word to be tenderhearted and forgiving toward one another, even as He is toward us. He sees all of our afflictions, and He wants us to treat others the same way we would want to be treated. Ephesians 4:32 says, "And be kind to one another, tenderhearted, forgiving one another, even as God in Christ forgave you." This is what we had to learn while taking care of all these boys. I did not have this kind of tenderheartedness naturally flowing out of me because of my upbringing. I remember that, when I was growing up, if one of us did something wrong, Mom would hold a grudge for a long time. She had a hard time with forgiveness. As a child, I never understood that, but I was determined to be more forgiving with the children that God had entrusted to us.

> *When God asks someone to do something, His request is also a promise to provide the wisdom and power required to fulfill His command*

Think about this: Through Jesus, God's love is revealed. By dying on the cross, He brought us as close to the Father and the Holy Spirit as we can get. I have heard it said that the pure unselfishness of God is revealed at the cross. This is where He makes His loving invitation to you. Come to Him to find the peace, understanding, and forgiveness you need to get through each day, particularly as you raise and care for His children.

Being a parent is the greatest kind of caregiving. God gives you beautiful children to bring up in His ways. When God asks someone to do something, His request is also a promise to provide the wisdom and power required to fulfill His command. God wants you to teach them according to His will, so that they will be saved for an eternity with Him. They will also teach their own children about the wonderful God we serve. Proverbs 22:6 says, "Train up a child in the way he should go, and when he is old he will not depart from it."

The True Meaning of Serving

For you, brethren, have been called to liberty; only do not use liberty as an opportunity for the flesh, but through love serve one another (Gal. 5:13).

All throughout my life, Jesus has been teaching me the lesson of how to serve others. After completing our year as dorm parents, God sent more exciting adventures to look forward to. Like the year we decided to move to Tennessee to be with our kids—that was an easy decision to make. Mark was out of work, and so there was nothing to keep us in Maine. We had raised our children for the Lord, providing them with a Christian education, and now they were all grown up and on their own. Two of them were attending a university in Tennessee, so making the decision to spend the school year near them seemed like a wonderful idea to me. That would mean I would get to be with my kids again for a while—a mother's dream come true! God opened all the necessary doors enabling us to go. Closing up the mobile home and packing our belongings, we started on our way, ready for anything in this new adventure!

We arrived in Tennessee full of joy and praise to God for giving us this opportunity. We stayed with some wonderful friends we knew until the kids found us a nice little house to rent. Now the only thing left to do was to find jobs. Mark and I both needed to work because of all the expenses that loomed before us. There was the mortgage for our home in Maine plus the monthly rental for the house in Tennessee. We were very thankful when Mark found a job at Spaulding Elementary Adventist School, working with computers.

During this time, our son Aaron and his German wife came from Germany to visit. We were delighted when they decided to look for a place to stay in America, especially since there was a baby on the way! They eventually found a house to rent not far from our home, which made me really happy. Now I felt our family was complete.

I was still looking for a job, and it was amazing to me to see the way God led. One day while I was at home alone, the phone rang. It was Aaron's landlord and she was looking for him. We got to talking, and I explained about my job search. She mentioned her mom, Phyllis, who was in need of a caregiver, and asked me if I would like to give it a try. Wow! I could not believe it! However, when she told me all the care her mom needed, I was not sure I could handle it. What a test God was about to give me—a test of serving others.

> **Think about this:** Jesus's whole life was about serving others. The profound example of this was at the Last Supper that Jesus had with His disciples, just before His crucifixion. He ordained the foot-washing service during the Last Supper. It was given to signify our renewed cleansing from sin, to offer us an opportunity to serve in Christ-like humility, and to bring us all together in love. He was trying to teach His disciples the true meaning of service.
>
> I would like to remind you of what Jesus did in that upper room at the Last Supper. He showed great love and humility to His disciples (John 13:3–10).[6] We are to do the same for one another.

Showing Christ's Love

A new commandment I give to you, that you love one another; as I have loved you, that you also love one another. By this all will know that you are My disciples, if you have love for one another (John 13:34, 35).

The night before starting my new job with Phyllis, I was feeling nervous and apprehensive. The list of things involved in caring for her seemed overwhelming. Having no nursing training, I did not know how to do half of what needed to be done. Her daughter assured me that she would teach me whatever I needed to know and thought everything would be fine. Nightmares engulfed me all that night, and, in the morning I was far from ready to begin this new chapter in my life.

I arrived at the appointed hour to meet Phyllis. She was eighty-two years old, and she was just as apprehensive of meeting me as I was of meeting her. She definitely had her own mind and knew how she wanted things done. Watching her, I decided this was not going to be an easy task! This would take some time, so I settled down to learn everything that I needed to know about how to care for her.

A few of the things were difficult, but eventually I was able to do them. She was bedridden, except for once a day when I had to place braces on her legs and get her up to try to walk. Placing the braces in the wrong position could injure her! What a responsibility on my shoulders! I prayed for God's help every morning. I was thankful that He gave me this job in spite of the hard work it required. He not only was teaching me the true meaning of serving others, but now there was enough money to take care of our expenses! God is awesome and knows just what our needs are, spiritually as well as monetarily.

Think about this: Jesus did not hesitate to serve others. We can do the same, asking for and receiving His sufficient grace. Being a caregiver sometimes entails doing some very hard things, but knowing Jesus did this—and more—for us, helps us trust Him to supply our need. Jesus lived a life of selfless service. He did not come to be served, but to serve (Matthew 20:28).[7] Washing His disciple's feet showed that He would do any service, no matter how lowly it was, to save a soul. In John 13:16, 17, it says, "Most assuredly, I say to you, a servant is not greater than his master; nor is he who is sent greater than he who sent him. If you know these things, blessed are you if you do them."

Always do your tasks happily, trying to be a witness to those souls who need you. Take time to be kind and compassionate through all the tough situations. Remember the pain they are going through and always do your best to be like Jesus. The Last Supper was given to show Christ's humility as a servant—something that we must learn to copy—as well as His love for others, even to the end (John 13:1).[8]

Reaping the Results

Why do you spend money for what is not bread, and your wages for what does not satisfy? Listen carefully to Me, and eat what is good, and let your soul delight itself in abundance (Isa. 55:2).

We spent some wonderful years living in Tennessee before it was time to return to Maine. My job was done with Phyllis, and I learned a lot during my time caring for her. I felt in my heart that God was preparing me for some day taking care of my own mother.

Being raised in an alcoholic home, I watched Mom and Dad and often wondered what was going to become of them as they grew older. Would they reap the results of living their unhealthy lifestyle? I was more worried about Dad with his smoking and drinking habits. I knew he could not go on as he had been without damaging his body. Mom did not smoke, and she drank very little. Her problem was with her eating habits. She did not eat very much, but she loved unhealthy, sugary things. She was a short woman who carried too much weight at times. Her blood pressure was too high, and she was on her way to becoming a diabetic. Dad, on the other hand, enjoyed his beer and cigarettes immensely. The smoking was causing problems with his lungs, but he refused to believe it.

Then came the day that Dad's lungs collapsed, and he had to be rushed to the hospital. From that day on his breathing became more difficult. His health went downhill and eventually he was bedridden. Mom had to care for him in the same way she had cared for her own mother. It was difficult for her to watch my dad wither away. He didn't want to go to the hospital, instead preferring Mom's care—which she did without any hesitation. All of us children were busy with our own lives and couldn't offer much help. Some lived too far away, and we all had jobs. The strain of taking care of dad was taking a toll on Mom's health as well.

Mother's Day came, and we were preparing to make the five-hour trip to Rhode Island to see them. Mom had just called me to say Dad was getting worse, and she did not feel he was going to be with us much longer. I asked her to place the phone by his ear so I could talk with him. When she did, I said, "I love you, Dad," and he responded to me in a whisper, just loud enough for me to hear. He said he knew. I continued to talk with him and said that we would be seeing him soon. In another low whisper, he said, "Okay."

As we were traveling, I kept praying that God would keep him alive so that we could be there with him. When we arrived, I went directly to his room. His eyes were closed and his breathing was shallow. I softly said, "We're here, Dad," as I took hold of his hand. At that moment, I sent up a prayer and asked God to let him go because he was suffering so much. Dad opened his eyes and looked directly at me. He knew I was there. He then closed his eyes for the last time. I thanked God that it was Mother's Day, and all of us kids were around Mom when she needed us most.

> *We do not live in a perfect world; there is sickness all around. Most diseases are preventable and are brought on ourselves by the choices we make. My parents did not make wise decisions when it came to their health*

Think about this: We do not live in a perfect world; there is sickness all around. Most diseases are preventable and are brought on ourselves by the choices we make. My parents did not make wise decisions when it came to their health, causing unnecessary caregiving on Mom's part. Let us rely on God to help us make the right choices, so we don't have to suffer needlessly or burden those we love.

God has promised to send the Holy Spirit to help us. In John 14:26, it says, "But the Helper, the Holy Spirit, whom the Father will send in My name, He will teach you all things, and bring to your remembrance all things that I said to you." If we could learn to rely on the strength of God, we would have so much more power within us. We forget that there are three distinct

Beings on our side: the Father, His Son Jesus, and the Holy Spirit. They are all working for us as one unit. John 10:30 says, "I and My Father are one," and John 14:16 says, "And I will pray the Father, and He will give you another Helper, that He may abide with you forever…." Pray that we never make the mistake of leaving Them out of our lives.

Mom

Trust in Him at all times, you people; Pour out your heart before Him; God is a refuge for us (Psalm 62:8).

Mom had a hard time adjusting to being alone after Dad's death. My son Aaron stayed with her for a while, which made her happy. However, he was still attending school and could not stay with her for long. Her eating habits were not good, and we worried about her all the time. Mom lived five hours away from us, but we visited as often as we could. I would clean the house and take care of some of her needs before heading back home. My sister and her husband lived close by—near enough to be there, if needed. My aunt took her shopping, which Mom enjoyed very much. We were all trying to do our part to take care of her, but she was not taking care of herself. It was only a matter of time before something drastic would happen.

I called Mom every morning and could usually tell by her voice how she was feeling. Many times she sounded sick and depressed. I tried to encourage her to go and see a doctor, but she refused to go no matter how bad she felt. Once, while we were talking on the phone, she kept coughing, and I asked her if she had a cold. She told me, "No," that it was just a bothersome cough. We didn't think much of it at the time, but, as her cough worsened, she finally agreed to go and see a doctor. Upon returning, she called me to say that they had found fluid in her lungs and around her heart. This was not good news, so Mark and I decided to make the five-hour trip to be with her. We found her in rough shape. Her legs and feet were swollen, and the cough still lingered. The simplest task, like coming to greet us at the door, was overwhelming for her. The medication the doctor prescribed was supposed to help remove the fluid, so all we could do was wait and see.

Mom was having other health issues. Sometimes when she stood up her balance was not good. We assumed it was because of the fluid in her legs and feet. The medication did not seem to be working. We urged her to go back to the doctor, but her answer was always, "No." We stayed with her for as long as we could, but finally we needed to go back home. We prayed together, then said our goodbyes. I felt in my heart it was not going to be long before she could not be left alone anymore. I prayed God would give us the strength to deal with whatever lay ahead for us.

Think about this: It is stressful for children to watch their parents' health decline after years of them making poor decisions concerning their health. I knew the outcome for Mom would not be good in the end, and, eventually, the results of making those poor decisions would come back on us kids. We loved Mom, and we were ready for whatever we had to do to keep her with us. If you are going through something like this, no matter what the reason, know that you are not alone. God does not promise to keep you from having all these trials, but He does promise to be with you through each ordeal. As God was with His dear Son while He hung on the cross, going through such agony, He will be with you, too. He is loving, faithful, just, and merciful.

The Stroke

*Fear not, for I am with you; be not dismayed, for I am your
God. I will strengthen you, yes, I will help you, I will uphold
you with My righteous right hand*
(Isa. 41:10).

It was Christmas time. Mark and I, along with our son, Andrew, decided to visit Mom for the holiday. Now that Dad was gone, she was alone most of the time, and she really did not care for that. My sister Millie and my brother did not live far away, only a half-hour drive. It would be a wonderful family holiday, visiting with everyone, and Mom would be so happy to see us. Mom seemed to be doing much better than she had in the past. The bothersome cough was gone, and her feet and legs were no longer swollen. However, she kept complaining of some dizziness.

On our last morning there, I was helping her by cleaning the house before we left. We worked together, getting the laundry done and fixing breakfast. Mom seemed to be in good spirits as we talked and laughed. We were finishing the last of the chores and making her bed, when she let out a scream and fell over. I ran to her side, calling to Mark for help. Mom could not walk, and her speech was slurred. But her mind was still clear, and she refused to let us call an ambulance. So instead, I called my sister, Millie, who is a nurse. She and her husband came over right away, and, upon examining her, Millie said Mom had suffered a stroke. We then called the ambulance, and they rushed her to the hospital. Our biggest fears concerning Mom and her health were finally coming to pass.

From that moment on, life changed for all of us. We were no longer thinking of going home, but about what should be done next. We were concerned about her welfare and started to ask questions like, "What is going to happen to Mom when she finally gets out of the hospital? Who is going to take care of her if she cannot be left alone anymore?"

Think about this: Have you found yourself in a similar situation? If you have, then you surely know how it feels to wonder if your loved one is going to die, along with the fear of trying to decide what the next step should be. It can be very devastating and exhausting to those involved.

Today, I want to be an encouragement to you by saying that we have a loving God who sees all you are going through and feels your pain. Place your trust in Him. He will not fail you. Won't you go to Him right now? He knows what is weighing heavily on your heart and mind. Go to His Word and claim this section's Scripture promise from Isaiah 41:10. Let His words give you the strength that you will need to face one day at a time. Remember, you are God's child. As a father watches over his children, so your Heavenly Father watches over you.

The Hospital

Who among you fears the Lord? Who obeys the voice of His Servant? Who walks in darkness and has no light? Let him trust in the name of the Lord and rely upon his God (Isaiah 50:10).

Following her stroke, we learned that Mom would remain in the rehab center of the hospital for at least five weeks. We extended our stay for several days until we found out where all this was headed. Even following the stroke, Mom was able to communicate with us. We explained that we had to return home, but we would keep in touch. We were not sure if Mom would ever be able to live in her own home.

With a heavy heart, we made the long trip back to our home. Everything had changed in just a few short days. We had driven to Mom's house with happy hearts, looking forward to a wonderful holiday. Now we were returning home with a sense of dread, not sure what the future held for any of us. Our joy had turned to deep concern for Mom's future. We were relieved to know that the stroke had not taken her life or her ability to communicate, but so many questions still hung over us. "What should we do to help Mom when her rehab center stay is over? Suppose she is still not well enough to live alone. Who could take care of her?" All of my brothers and sisters worked each day and would not be able to provide the personal daily care she needed so much.

> *We all face hard decisions and some sort of crisis at one point or another in our lives. It isn't easy to travel these paths alone*

It began to dawn on me that I'd be responsible for Mom's care, since I was not working at the time. But we lived so far from her home and her doctors. How would we handle the situation? The question whirled in my brain. Would this mean that I would have to leave my husband for a while. I realized that all we could do was to pray and leave the whole situation to God.

> **Think about this:** We all face hard decisions and some sort of crisis at one point or another in our lives. It isn't easy to travel these paths alone. When you are struggling with questions and your way seems unclear, know that God's Son, Jesus, understands all that you are going through. Today, if you are the one facing a difficult task, look at this section's Scripture again. Jesus came to this earth and became a servant for others. Humbling Himself, He ministered to every need. He wants you to do the same. Rely on God to lead you in the right direction. You are not alone. Others are in similar situations, and they can provide encouragement or advice. But, most importantly, God, through His Son, will be your light in the darkest night. Just look to Him for help and wisdom, and He will guide your every step.

Bringing Mom Home

*O God, do not be far from me; O my God,
make haste to help me!* (Ps. 71:12)

A few weeks after Mom's stroke, we again drove the five hours to see her. We had been in contact with Mom and my siblings regularly, and we knew she was recovering well except for her ability to walk. Her speech had improved, and she was alert and impatient to return home. She really disliked the rehab center and did not eat very well while she was there.

Upon our arrival there, we found Mom whipping around in a wheelchair, and I mean whipping around! She knew how to get around well in that chair! After taking one look at her big, bright, alert eyes, I knew she was ready to leave the rehab center! However, her doctors wanted her to stay a few more days. The physical therapist told me that once Mom went home, she would need to return every day to continue her physical therapy to help regain her balance. The doctor had told us that her stroke had damaged the part of the brain that enables her to balance and walk. He said she might never be able to walk again. He didn't know Mom very well! She was a determined woman, and nothing was going to keep her down for long.

After each rehab visit with Mom, Mark and I would go to her apartment and try to get it ready for her to return home. That was not an easy task because the apartment was small and crowded—not a great place for someone just learning to walk again. We removed her scatter rugs because of the tripping danger they created, and we bought all the necessary rehab-related things that she would need—like a walker, a portable toilet, a cane, and more! Finally, with everyday things positioned safely and the rehab-related equipment in place, we went to get her. We knew that I had a big job ahead of me if I was going to take care of Mom, a job that would take a lot of patience and prayer to meet the challenges of each new day. Mom was used to doing things on her own, and now she would have to rely on me.

Think about this: We all cherish our independence, and, if the time ever comes when we have to rely on our children or someone else to take care of us, it will not be easy. This transition is hard for the caregiver, as well as for the one being cared for. Take another look at this section's Scripture verse and pray over it. Trust that God will be by your side, bringing you safely through every challenge you have to face. He was there for me when I needed Him. He will be there for you, too. Through His Son, Jesus, you will learn to have genuine love, joy, peace, longsuffering, kindness, goodness, faithfulness, gentleness, and self-control (Gal. 5:22, 23).[9]

Physical Therapy

Then they cried out to the Lord in their trouble, and
He saved them out of their distresses (Ps. 107:13).

Living with and caring for Mom was different from what I was used to. The physical therapist came to her home once a week (instead of every day) to work with her, and so I would help her do her exercises in between those visits. It seemed Mom was regaining her strength little by little. Eventually, the physical therapist was no longer needed. I was on my own, helping her with her exercises five times a day to help her walk again. I was thankful for the long railing in the hallway of her apartment building. Mom and I would go into the hall, where she could hold onto that bar while she exercised and practiced walking. She was making great progress, despite the doctor's prediction that she would never be able to walk again!

Every morning, Mom and I would start our day with God, reading from the Bible and praying together. Then we would have our breakfast and head out into the hallway to start her exercise routine. Our afternoons were filled with games, talking, and just sharing time with each other. Those were very special times.

Everything seemed to be going very well, but I noticed that Mom's cataracts were impairing her vision and slowing her recovery. I urged her to have cataract surgery, but she refused. The fear of doctors got the better of her, so she simply pushed aside my suggestion and said, "I can live with this."

Mom enjoyed having me live with her. She was no longer feeling alone, but I wanted to get home to my husband! I wondered if that was ever going to happen. Mark drove the long trip to be with us as often as he could. I knew our separation was as hard on him as it was on me.

Then Mom fell, hurting her leg and delaying her exercise time and progress. As the weeks dragged on, I found myself crying and praying to God for help with the situation. As far as I could see there was no end in sight. Trying to handle this heavy burden on my own was weighing me down. I had to trust that God was not far away from me and that, as hopeless as it seemed, things were going to get better.

> **Think about this:** If you are feeling weighed down and thinking there is no hope, remember that you are serving a great God. He knows all you are going through, and He is standing beside you, holding you up and welcoming you into His presence with open arms. Come to Him on your knees and pour out all of your distress. Ask Him to send the Holy Spirit, our Helper and Comforter, to give you peace (John 16:7).[10]

Waiting for God's Answer

*Hear my prayer, O Lord, give ear to my supplications! In
Your faithfulness answer me, and in Your righteousness*
(Ps. 143:1).

Mom's injured leg was getting better, so we resumed her exercise program. Each day that went by left me feeling more and more alone and missing my husband terribly. I was thankful he was still able to come and see us on the weekends, but traveling five hours after working hard all week was taking a big toll on him. I loved being with Mom, but I needed to be home with my husband.

Then, one evening, the phone rang. It was a call from Mark. He explained that he was going to fly to Virginia to interview for a new job. Excitement mounted in me as he was speaking! Suppose they hired him! It would mean a big move for us! Mark was ready for a change, and the Lord knew I was ready, too. Could this be the answer to my prayers, the change that we all so desperately needed?

Later that week, Mark called to say that he had gotten the job. I was excited beyond words, but wondered what to do with Mom. She was still not well enough to live by herself, and I needed to return home to pack for my big move. We were facing another challenge, but I knew where to find the answer. I went to my knees asking for guidance and praying for the Holy Spirit to show us the way. It seemed we were hitting a wall, but God was teaching me patience, and it was not an easy lesson for me to learn!

> **Think about this:** When you find yourself hitting a wall, and there doesn't seem to be anywhere to turn, tell it to Jesus. He loves to listen, and He will provide you with a way out through the guidance of His Holy Spirit. This can only happen in God's time, not yours.

The hardest thing you will have to do is to wait for His answer. Rest assured it will come. He never fails us. We fail Him when we become impatient and want an answer now. By doing that, we are not giving God a chance to answer. This section's Scripture assures you, He is faithful. He will send you the Helper, and, when He does, the results will be far better than anything you could do on your own.

Life-Changing Decisions

But let patience have its perfect work, that you may be perfect and complete, lacking nothing (James 1:4).

I needed to return home and prepare for our move, so I called my brother and asked if he could take care of Mom until we were ready to take her to our new home. After talking to his family, he told me they would come and care for Mom until we could get settled. We were relieved and happy, but Mom was not. She did not want to leave her home, and the realization of possibly losing everything she treasured was weighing heavily on her. She had to come to terms with the fact that living alone might no longer be an option. In light of all that, there were many last-minute things to do before we could even think about going to our new home in Virginia. Mom still had the hope of returning to her apartment someday. We decided it would be best to keep her apartment for a short time, just to see where things would lead. We both knew better, but neither of us wanted to admit it. Ignoring the facts was easier than facing reality.

Let us look at one another through the eyes of God; not just seeing someone who is in our way as being a burden, but as someone who is fearfully and wonderfully made by His loving hands

It is so hard for an aging person who is about ready to lose everything he or she loves. Mom cried for a very long time. I tried hard to put myself in her shoes, trying to understand what she was going through. For the most part, I was thinking of myself and my own happiness and not really giving a lot of thought to what Mom was feeling. I had a hard time understanding why she wasn't accepting the decisions we were making on her behalf.

God surely had to teach me about kindness and consideration. It was another hard lesson to learn.

In this section's Scripture, God asks us to be patient and He promises we will not lack in anything. His grace will help us be kind and understanding toward one another. God was constantly trying to teach me patience, and I had to learn how to be thankful while going through all these trials.

Think about this: When you are faced with life-changing events concerning the elderly, try to put yourself in their place and imagine how they might be feeling. Always remember to respect the life God has given to us because it is His greatest gift. We were created in God's image. The spirit of compassion should flow easily as we see our fellow humans suffering. Being formed in His image should give us a better understanding of the worth of each person. God cares because we are His children. Mankind is His glorious masterpiece. I had lots more lessons to learn about how to treat another human being. Let us look at one another through the eyes of God; not just seeing someone who is in our way as being a burden, but as someone who is fearfully and wonderfully made by His loving hands (Ps. 139:14).[11]

Leaving Mom

Then He who sat on the throne said, "Behold, I make all things new." And He said to me, "Write, for these words are true and faithful" (Rev. 21:5).

Everything seemed to be going well since my brother's phone call. Mom was starting to accept the fact that she would be leaving her home in a little while to stay with my brother and his family. Her walking was improving daily. She was now using the "hated cane," as she referred to it, and she was determined to start walking alone with nothing for support. Every day, she tried harder to accomplish this task. How different things were compared to a few short months ago when the doctor had told her she would never walk again. God certainly had a different outcome in mind!

My brother contacted us to say when he would make the trip with his family. I called Mark and told him when to come and pick me up. It turned out that everyone would be arriving at the same time, and my excitement escalated! It was hard for me to wait, and, again, I had to exercise patience. To pass the time, Mom and I started to pack and get ready for her big move. Was I detecting a little excitement in Mom as we did the packing? She actually was starting to look forward to the trip!

We were still making final preparations on the day everyone was to arrive. Excitement was in the air, no question about it! There wasn't a thing that could happen to discourage me, and we would be seeing everyone soon! When they came, we had a wonderful visit. Then came the time for Mom to say goodbye and leave on the sixteen-hour trip to my brother's home. We promised her that it would only be a month until we would be together again. She seemed in good spirits, but I knew she was leaving with a heavy heart. I watched as she was saying her goodbyes. I saw the pain in her eyes as she relived all the memories that apartment held of her children and grandchildren visiting and of Dad sitting in the corner watching television. That place represented her independence. Looking around one last time, there was a realization in her mind that she might not be returning.

When I think back to that moment, watching Mom say goodbye to everything she had held close to her heart for so many years, I can feel the loss and emptiness she must have been experiencing as she looked around her home one last time. These were all the memories that made Mom who she was. It was a joyous day for me, but a sad one for Mom.

> **Think about this:** Are we conscious of one another? Do we feel the sorrow of elderly persons about to lose everything they hold dear? I know God does. He sees what's going on in their hearts and minds. He wants us to show compassion for His children as they go through difficult phases in their lives. We are to treat them as we would want to be treated if the roles were reversed and we were the ones saying goodbye, losing our independence, and having to rely on our families.
>
> Will you know what to do and say when you face these hard trials? Go to God's word for comfort and lean on the promise that Jesus will be coming again to make all things new. We will never have to say goodbye again. How we long for the day when He will create a whole new world without sorrow or pain. Everything God does is motivated by His great love for us. We are the children of His love. Just as He created the world so long ago—with all the care and concern and love for His creation—He will not fail to do it again. Psalm 33:6 says, "By the word of the Lord the heavens were made, and all the host of them by the breath of His mouth."

Making Preparations

*This also comes from the Lord of hosts, Who is wonderful
in counsel and excellent in guidance*
(Isa. 28:29).

Mom was on her way to my brother's home, and it was time to head back to my own home. There was a big job awaiting us there. The company that hired Mark was sending movers to move our things, and I wanted to be there to make sure everything was done correctly. I had only a month to move and then get things ready for Mom to come and move in with us in our new home. My husband's new company stored our belongings and provided a temporary, furnished place for us to live. However, the place they chose was on the second floor! There was no way Mom was going to be able to climb all those stairs. When we asked the company for a first-floor apartment and explained that my mother was coming to live with us, they kindly agreed.

We were still praying and searching for a home of our own. The company had agreed to pay for the apartment and storage of our things for a specific length of time, and our time was running out. It was difficult to find anything we could afford, so we decided to remain in the apartment and bring Mom to live with us there. Mom was very happy to be coming home with us, but I wanted to be in a permanent place before she came. We prayed about it, but it seemed that God was saying, "Not yet." I had to trust Him that everything would work out in His time, not mine.

We made the long drive to my brother's home to bring Mom to her new home with us. It was an exciting time of change, but we had no idea how difficult it was going to be adjusting to one another.

Think about this: Have you ever found yourself at a loss over what to do next—like having a huge responsibility and not being ready for it at all? When everything seems to be unknown and nothing is going the way you planned it, all you can do is pray and rely on God! This section's Scripture says that He is wonderful in counsel and guidance. Trust in Him for all your answers. I had to wait and listen for His counsel. At times, that was not easy, but I made it through one day at a time, and so will you.

Mom Moves In

*Trust in the Lord, and do good; dwell in the land, and feed
on His faithfulness* (Ps. 37:3).

Adjusting to life with Mom proved to be very difficult. She did not seem to be the same person we had left just a month ago. Before leaving to stay with my brother, there was still the hope of her getting better and living on her own again. Now, she knew for sure that was not going to happen, and it changed her. She was stubborn in many ways. One of the hardest things I had to deal with was her eating habits. I was at a total loss as to what to do. I tried to remember that she was not a child, but the fear of her getting sick was weighing heavily on me. Arguing over food was not the way I wanted to witness to her, and it did not benefit either of us. When I finally gave it over to God, I was able to come to terms with her eating habits. That seemed to make things better, and, as a result, the fighting stopped.

> *When God gives you a responsibility that seems to be overwhelming in every way and there is nowhere to turn, the Scriptures are a place to go for encouragement*

We still had to deal with the need to move again soon. The month that the company had given us was almost over. It was hard to find a place we could afford. Nothing was working out, and, on top of it all, Mom's apartment still had to be packed up, which meant we had to rent another storage place here in Virginia. We made arrangements for my son Tim and a few of his friends to go and clean out her apartment. This did not prove to be an easy task because of the amount of things in her apartment. They finally managed to finish the job and were able to bring back everything to Virginia. With that out of the way, we could put our efforts into finding a more permanent place to live. Having Mom in our apartment made it more complicated to get things done, but we had to go on and have faith that God would lead us in the right direction.

I felt as if my plate was overflowing. I would cry, thinking it was too much for Him to ask of me, especially when I did not feel ready to accept this new responsibility. Not having a permanent place to live and trying to deal with Mom at the same time was proving to be too much. I had to totally rely on God and trust Him completely. What else could I do? I either had to trust Him or give up, but I couldn't give up for the sake of Mom and my husband!

> **Think about this:** When God gives you a responsibility that seems to be overwhelming in every way and there is nowhere to turn, the Scriptures are a place to go for encouragement. Psalm 37:3, this section's Scripture, tells us to feed on God's faithfulness. Every time you see that old nature of yours popping up—wanting to gratify self or trying to find the easy way out—go to your knees and search your heart. God, through the Holy Spirit, will guide you.
>
> Remember that you are a fallen human being, sinful by nature. We are born weak and have a tendency to do evil, but, through Christ and His Spirit, we are brought back and restored to our original nature, which is the character of God. We are called by Him to love one another and to care for all things. The only hope of being delivered from that fallen nature is to go to Jesus just as you are, asking for forgiveness and to be changed into His character. It is His delight to do that for you!

Learning to Trust

*Then you shall call, and the Lord will answer; you shall cry,
and He will say, 'Here I am'* (Isa. 58:9).

Every day, I was learning to feed on God's faithfulness. Mom and I were starting to enjoy each other, and it felt like old times again. We were still praying for God to find us the perfect place to move to. It had to be big enough for two families. Even though Mom was just one person, she needed her own living room, bedroom, and bathroom. The number of her belongings was overwhelming, and she did not want to part with any of them. I worked hard to abide by her wishes. Having already done a lot of adjusting to make this move, Mom didn't need any more stress; I did not want to add any more stress. I also knew seeing all of her belongings again would make her happy.

But we needed answers soon, because time was getting short. Feeling desperate, we put a deposit on an apartment, even though I was concerned about the size of it. I did not think all of our things would fit in it. Also, it was not close by, and it would take many trips to move all of our belongings there, using just our car. This was not a good situation for us, but what could we do? That problem would have to be dealt with later. Sad to say, we were reacting to the pressure of our situation and not seeking God's will for us.

One day, after making our deposit on the new apartment, we all decided to go out for a drive; we came across a nice neighborhood with beautiful homes. Mom and I began daydreaming about what it would be like to live in one of those! Driving along, Mark spotted a "For Rent" sign in front of a two-story house. Liking the looks of it, we stopped and called the telephone number on the sign in the yard. A woman answered. I told her of our interest and asked about seeing the inside. She said it was not possible just then, but for us to go home and check our e-mail. She would post some pictures, and, if we were still interested, we could call her back when her husband was home. I quickly gave her my e-mail address and hung up.

Oh, what excitement! We could hardly wait to see those pictures! It did not take long before they arrived in our e-mail. The house seemed to be perfect. There were two and a half baths and two living rooms, which would be great for us. One of the bedrooms was connected to a living room, and a half bath, which would give Mom her own space! Now all that was left for us to do was to talk with the landlord.

After finalizing things with him, we were still faced with trying to get our deposit back from the other apartment. They had made it clear to us earlier that it would not be an easy thing to do. We were praying again for a much-needed miracle. I called them and was surprised when they gladly refunded our deposit. How thankful we were that God had heard and answered our prayers, even when we had not waited for His guidance! He was well aware of all our needs. It wasn't long before we were moving in to God's choice for our home!

> **Think about this:** God knows just what your needs are without you telling Him, but He loves to hear from His children! He wants you to rely totally on Him. Attempting to do things on your own only gives Satan the ability to exercise his will over you. After Jesus's baptism, He went to the wilderness to fast and pray. There He was tempted by Satan to doubt that He was the Son of God. During His weakest moments of hunger and fatigue, Satan came and tried to have Him rely on His own power to change stones into bread (Matt. 4:3) instead of trusting in God's timing. Satan was trying to cause Christ to doubt God's word which He, the Father, had spoken at His baptism, saying, "...This is My beloved Son, in whom I am well pleased" (Matt. 3:17). There is a great controversy going on between good and evil, God and Satan. Let us say, as Jesus did in answer to Satan's attack, "Man shall not live by bread alone, but by every word that proceeds from the mouth of God....Away with you, Satan" (Matt. 4:4, 10).

Combining Lives

Love suffers long and is kind; love does not envy; love does not parade itself, is not puffed up; does not behave rudely, does not seek its own, is not provoked, thinks no evil; does not rejoice in iniquity, but rejoices in the truth; bears all things, believes all things, hopes all things, endures all things (1 Cor. 13:4–7).

Once we had a home, we began packing our belongings to get ready for the move! Our first stop was Mom's storage unit. The anticipation of seeing her belongings again caused her great joy. We arranged for my husband's company to deliver the storage pod that held all of our belongings to our new home. The house was move-in ready, making our move so much easier. Mom and I were both going to be happy to see all of our things once again!

Combining two households into one was not going to be easy. Mom and I had very different tastes and ideas. Mark, on the other hand, stayed neutral. He wasn't going to get between two women, no matter what we decided—a wise decision! The only request he had was to give him room enough to walk—a path through all the clutter until we could find a permanent place for everything. We couldn't argue with that!

Despite a lot of tug of wars between Mom and me, all was shaping up nicely. Because it was a good-sized house, everything eventually fit without looking crowded. Mom seemed content and really loved her own space because it was almost like being in her own home again.

> **Think about this:** The biggest concern of the elderly is the fear of losing everything they love. Some have already lost their loved ones, possibly their homes, and finally—most of all— they lose their independence. Not all are lucky enough to keep their possessions as Mom did. God wants us to understand what the

elderly are going through and to be patient, loving, and kind to them. It's never easy to combine two lives. Always remember to have good manners toward one another. This will help you get along. Read this section's Scripture and refresh your mind as to what love is.

Remember you are not alone. God is on one side representing love, and Satan is on the other side, trying to do everything contrary to it. Ephesians 6:12 says, "For we do not wrestle against flesh and blood, but against principalities, against powers, against the rulers of the darkness of this age, against spiritual hosts of wickedness in the heavenly places." Ephesians 6:13 says, "Therefore take up the whole armor of God, that you may be able to withstand in the evil day, and having done all, to stand." Understanding fully this great controversy will give you hope and courage as you face the future, knowing Jesus is in control. Our victory is assured!

God's Way

*As for God, His way is perfect; the word of the Lord is
proven; He is a shield to all who trust in Him*
(2 Sam. 22:31).

A year went by and we were still enjoying our new home. When we had a chance to visit our children in Germany, my brother and his wife offered to take care of Mom so that we could go. Knowing she was in safe hands, we could relax and have some fun with our grandchild. Also, Mom and I needed some time apart. The separation proved to be good for all of us, and we appreciated each other even more upon our return.

> **I tend to run ahead of God without waiting for Him to answer my prayers. Each time I learned one lesson, there was always another one waiting for me**

Then, one dreadful day, we received a phone call from our landlord telling us that the owner of the house was going to sell! Our hearts sank with disappointment. He asked if we would consider purchasing it, but the price was beyond our means. The thought of moving again was daunting. Mom was devastated because, at her age, she needed stability. We found ourselves praying for guidance again, not understanding why this was happening. We were trying our best to do what was right. So many times I asked God, "Why? You know that I have Mom, and it is not easy to make such a big move with her." God had His reasons, and I would have to trust His judgment, but my moving again was not going to be with a willing heart.

I called a realtor to help us look for another house. Again and again, we went out looking for a suitable place to live. She even suggested getting some land and placing a modular home on it. That excited us to think that maybe this was the answer! Pursuing that path, we found some land and proceeded to pick out our modular home. Mom and I spent many hours daydreaming about it.

A lot of people came to see the house we were renting. One couple made an offer on it, and they wanted to move in soon—long before we could finalize our plan for a new home. We would have to find another temporary place to live!

Again, desperation darkened our doorstep, and, without any hesitation we started looking around without the realtor. Nothing looked promising. On our way home, we noticed a "For Rent" sign in front of an apartment building near our current home! We had passed that place hundreds of times. How could we have missed seeing that sign? Stopping to check it out, we learned that there was a first-floor apartment available, and it was within our price range. The apartment was small, and so the move would not be so stressful. But we would have to store a lot of our things in another storage unit. We hoped we wouldn't have to remain in the apartment for long.

> **Think about this:** I tend to run ahead of God without waiting for Him to answer my prayers. Each time I learned one lesson, there was always another one waiting for me. Do you find yourself doing that? Hurrying blindly in one direction, you do not see something that is right in front of your eyes. Our prayer should always be, "Teach me Thy way, O Lord" (Ps. 86:11, KJV). God's way is always the best way. We have a Savior who died for us. He is interested in all our activities. He has an everlasting love for His children. Jeremiah 31:3 says, "The Lord has appeared of old to me, saying: Yes, I have loved you with an everlasting love; therefore with lovingkindness I have drawn you."

This section's Scripture tells us to trust Him because His way is perfect. He is our example. We can do nothing good or wise on our own. Isaiah 64:6 says, "But we are all like an unclean thing, and all our righteousnesses are like filthy rags; we all fade as a leaf, and our iniquities, like the wind, have taken us away." Christ clothes us with His robe of righteousness. Isaiah 61:10 says, "I will greatly rejoice in the Lord, my soul shall be joyful in my God; for He has clothed me with the garments of salvation, He has covered me with the robe of righteousness, as a bridegroom decks himself with ornaments, and as a bride adorns herself with her jewels." We are made perfect only through Christ's life, death, and resurrection. Let us wait patiently for the guidance of the Lord. He knows the way; all we have to do is follow Him.

Disappointment

It is better to trust in the Lord than to put confidence in man (Ps. 118:8).

Preparing to leave our beautiful house brought a heavy sadness to our hearts. We had enjoyed our year there and had made it our home. The small apartment was nothing compared to the house. The only bright spot in this whole ordeal was that we knew it would not be permanent. The downside was that we could take only the things that would fit. We rented a storage unit for our big items. Everything else would be taken in the car and a small trailer behind it that Mark built. The house was emptied, and we had to say our goodbyes.

The dreamed-for home on our land didn't work out, and we were once again disappointed. We were trying to trust in God to help us make the right decisions, and so we didn't understand why all of these setbacks were happening. It felt as if our efforts were crumbling, but God was teaching us to take it slow and stop trusting in our own efforts to make our lives better.

My selfish heart still wanted to say, "If only we did not have Mom, things would be easier to face." Trying to please her was so difficult sometimes. She was unhappy about having to move into another small apartment and part with her belongings yet again. Well, so were we! I tried to place myself in her shoes, but that was not easy to do.

Think about this: Sometimes one obstacle after another seems to arise when you are trying to do your best. We have to remember that Jesus sees the future clearly. He wants you to give yourself totally to Him. When you do that, those huge obstacles will melt, and your pathway will become clear to walk on.

Do not look to humans for your answers, but look only to the One Who truly has an interest in what you are doing—the One

Who has laid down His life for you. John 10:15 says, "As the Father knows Me, even so I know the Father; and I lay down My life for the sheep." We are Christ's sheep.

Jesus knows our weaknesses, and He understands. Hebrews 4:15 says, "For we do not have a High Priest who cannot sympathize with our weaknesses, but was in all points tempted as we are, yet without sin." Let us look only to our risen Savior and say with the apostle Paul, "I can do all things through Christ who strengthens me" (Phil. 4:13). Look to Jesus for your deliverance. He's right by your side.

Clothed in God's Righteousness

For He made Him who knew no sin to be sin for us, that we might become the righteousness of God in Him
(2 Cor. 5:21).

Living in a small apartment was proving to be very hard at times for the three of us. Mark's office was crammed into the laundry room, and, when he came home from work, he would go in there to enjoy the solitude. This allowed him to be away from Mom and I—two stressful women who could drive him crazy. Unlike me, Mark usually went along with everything. When I think back on those times, it seemed I was always annoyed with Mom. I wonder what really caused all my annoyance. She never did anything serious to warrant it. I realize now how much I needed a transformation of mind and heart, and it would not have hurt to have had more room.

Life in the apartment was not going to work for very long. We decided to call the realtor again, with the intent of buying a home instead of renting. The realtor came, and we went out looking every day. I always said, "When the right house comes along, I will know it," but that just didn't seem to be happening. We looked at house after house. There were suitable ones that would fit our little family's needs nicely, but they just didn't seem right in other ways.

One day, the realtor called to say she had just the house for us! It was not even on the market yet, but it was located in a particular city. My heart sank, because I did not want to live in that city. It was crowded, and it was not at all what I envisioned for us. We had always lived in nice, quiet, and peaceful little towns. This city bustled with so many people and cars. Despite my doubts, we decided to look at the area where she told us the house was located.. We couldn't tour the house because the owners had not yet put it up for sale. As we drove closer to where the house was, I started getting excited! The neighborhood was really nice! The front yard was well kept, and the house appeared to be everything I wanted! I felt God was telling me this was the one! However, when we finally were able to look inside, I questioned God and His judgment. The house was a disaster, with holes in the walls and damaged doors. The carpets smelled of urine, and I just couldn't see the potential! I cried to God, asking, "What were You thinking?" Again, in the days to come, God showed me that His plans are perfect and that I would be happy.

> **Think about this:** This house represented me in my present state of mind regarding taking care of Mom. Just as this house needed major attention and repairs, I needed Christ's righteousness. I, too, was full of holes and badly in need of repair. Like Joshua (Zech. 3:1, 2), I stood before the Angel of the Lord clothed in filthy rags. Satan was calling for my condemnation, and he is right—I am a big sinner. His accusations were correct, but God, in His divine mercy, takes away my filthy garments and clothes me with the robe of Christ's righteousness.
>
> Zechariah 3:1–4.[12] I am an undeserving, repentant sinner, but God helps me to experience forgiveness and to be purified of my sins. This is the experience of justification that we all need in order to be adopted into the family of God and live forever in His kingdom.

Reaching the Goal

Not that I have already attained, or am already perfected; but I press on, that I may lay hold of that for which Christ Jesus has also laid hold of me....I press toward the goal for the prize of the upward call of God in Christ Jesus (Phil. 3:12, 14).

The new house we were looking at was not far from Williamsburg, a tourist town, which meant the crime rate was lower. I felt in my heart that this area would be a great place to live. The neighbors were so nice, and the area seemed peaceful. I felt convicted that this house was God's choice for us, and so I just had to look past all the repairs and see the potential that God saw. The backyard was just as messy as the inside of the house! It needed cleaning up, and some trees would need to be cut down in order to see the real beauty, but there was a wonderful, good-sized deck. The yard was big and fenced in, which was an answer to my prayer. This home met all of our criteria, and God knew it.

As soon as we were able to move in, we began knocking down walls, repairing holes, and painting—not to mention all the cleaning that had to be done. After finishing, we were able to step back and see how really beautiful this house was. What a change! It was home at last!

> *As we rolled up our sleeves and worked on the house, I realized that this renovation mirrored what God needed to do in my life: transform my ugly, selfish ways into something that was beautiful*

As we rolled up our sleeves and worked on the house, I realized that this renovation mirrored what God needed to do in my life: transform my ugly, selfish ways into something that was beautiful. My character needed a renewal, especially when it came to taking care of my mom. At times, I would only think of myself and what I wanted, rather than thinking of Mom and her needs—never wondering how she might be feeling, sitting day after day in that big mess while we were doing the repairs. It had to have been upsetting to her. God showed me the errors of my ways.

> **Think about this:** As God's caregiver, you are given the opportunity to care for another life, to care about what is going on in that person's mind and heart. You need to behold Christ working, not only in the life of the person you are caring for, but in your own life as well. Even if the person you care for does not choose to submit to God's transformation, you can choose to let Him change you into His likeness. This sanctification takes a lifetime to accomplish. Let us press on toward the goal of spending eternity with Jesus!

The Beautiful Light

*He has delivered us from the power of darkness and
conveyed us into the kingdom of the Son of His love...*
(Col. 1:13).

After months of arduous work, our new home was finished and looking very sweet as we settled down to enjoy it. Mom and I were still having trouble adjusting to each other, even after being together for an entire year. Her cataracts burdened her with poor eyesight, but the ever-present fear of doctors overpowered her desire to see well. Her deteriorating vision put her in serious danger. She had a hard time walking due to the stroke and her cataracts, and it was getting more and more difficult for her to do everyday things. Reaching for a cup of tea, she would misjudge the distance and spill the contents. We often spent hours playing games to keep her mind busy, but eventually that fun activity had to stop because her vision had deteriorated so much. Something had to be done—right away.

We argued over this problem quite often, and life was becoming unbearable for both of us. At last I put my foot down, and she finally agreed to see a doctor about her cataracts.

What a happy day it was when she was able to see clearly in both eyes. It was a whole new world to her! The danger of her falling was no longer an issue. We were praising God for this miracle, and life in the LaPierre home was great again.

Then an awful thing happened. An infection settled in one of her eyes, and we had to go back to the doctor to get it checked. Unfortunately, it could not be treated, and Mom lost her sight in that eye. I could not understand why God allowed that to happen when we had made such an effort to help her regain her eyesight. I had to remember how all things work together for good to those who love the Lord (Rom. 8:28).[13] There was a reason for it, and some day we will know what it was. We just had to accept it and thank God for that she had at least one good eye.

Think about this: We all have "spiritual cataracts" that cause us to live in darkness, fearful of the future. Pray every day for God to remove your "spiritual cataracts." I remember the day Mom's vision was restored. She was walking all around the house, saying, "Wow, I can see!" What a difference it makes to be able to "see the light." As the hymn "Amazing Grace" says, "I...was blind, but now I see."* God is the Great Physician who can help you see the light and have the compassion you need.

*Newton, John. "Amazing Grace." *The Seventh-day Adventist Hymnal*. Hagerstown, MD: Review and Herald Publishing Association, 1985, p. 108.

Leaning on Jesus

But grow in the grace and knowledge of our Lord and Savior Jesus Christ. To Him be the glory both now and forever. Amen (2 Peter 3:18).

Now that Mom was able to see, life was pretty sweet for a while. We were starting to enjoy each other again. We would play games in the afternoons, and she seemed happy. Then came the day we were told that she was a diabetic. Oh my, another challenge! Mom was devastated! Having to rely on someone all the time was not her idea of a good life, and now she would really have to depend on me to administer her insulin shots. In her mind, her life was over. Depression set in, and she soon found herself taking medication for that as well.

Whatever the task is that is facing you, make it an opportunity to learn to lean on Jesus

I was questioning God again. Why were bad things always happening to Mom? She had all kinds of issues already without adding more stress. Unfortunately, I could see that she was reaping the results of her past deeds—of eating too many sweets for too many years. She always requested junk food whenever I shopped for her, and I always listened to what she wanted. I tried to tell her to be careful, but she was a very independent woman, and I had little influence over her. I was thankful that she was still able to take care of her own needs, such as bathing and cooking. It all could have been so much worse. I had to remind myself of that every day. Even though Mom did not require a lot of care, my compassion was still needed to deal with all the challenges that came our way. Some of those challenges were not small ones. One day, there was a big lump on her neck that burst! What fear she felt when that happened! Then, other lumps began appearing on her body, including by her eyes. I was fearful that one of those lumps near her good eye would cause her to go blind. Several doctors were stymied by her condition, and it continued to worsen. She was discouraged and embarrassed by her skin lesions. Life for Mom was getting worse, and sometimes that would make us both miserable.

I had to keep giving Mom's situation to Jesus, asking Him to set us free from all these burdens. I found myself on my knees praying for guidance, trying to be as cheerful as I could whenever Mom and I were together. I needed strength to focus on the good, not the bad. And it was not easy. I could not have done it without Jesus helping me. Praying helped me see things in a better state of mind.

There were times when Mom was grateful to my husband and me for our faithful care. I did love her, despite all the challenges we faced together.

> **Think about this:** We are to show God's love for everyone by the service we do for one another, as we witness to His salvation. Whatever the task is that is facing you, make it an opportunity to learn to lean on Jesus. No burden—nothing—is too heavy for Him.

God's Family

But if we walk in the light as He is in the light, we have fellowship with one another, and the blood of Jesus Christ His Son cleanses us from all sin (1 John 1:7).

Mom was finally accepting and getting used to her health conditions, and life was beginning to feel normal around our home. I learned how to take good care of her, but she still needed medication for depression every day. We loved going to church. Mom would come with us, despite the embarrassment of her skin condition, because she did not like being alone. I was grateful for that, always hoping to be a good witness to her. There were many churches in the area of our new home. No matter which one we attended, there were caring people who treated us as family.

One of the churches we attended was having communion. I was not too sure what Mom would think. I was pleased when she partook of the service, including the foot washing. It just thrilled me to be able to do that with her! We were only able to do it together just that once in my lifetime, but I will always remember that day.

Mom eventually stopped going to church with us because of those embarrassing lumps. They finally got the better of her. What a sad day that was for us because I loved it when she would come and be a part of everything. The people in the church would not have cared about those lumps; they would have just cared about her and would have extended the right hand of fellowship to her.

A church is a place where each person is loved, respected, and recognized as somebody—a place where you can grow spiritually with one another. When Mom stopped attending church, she missed out on an extended family who would have loved and encouraged her in the same way that Christ loves us. Being left alone all the time while we went to worship and fellowship was very sad for her, but for us to miss church and stay with her was not an option. That would not have been good for any of us, especially when round-the-clock care was not needed yet. I needed the spiritual blessings that worship brought. Many caregivers cannot leave their post to attend church to receive a spiritual blessing, and that is hard on them.

> **Think about this:** If you are one of those caregivers who cannot leave your charge alone, I encourage you to find a church, and then invite some of the people from church to come and visit you. It will be a blessing to you as well as the one you are caring for. There were several church members who would occasionally come to visit Mom during the week. She eventually started to love them and looked forward to their visits. It did wonders for her. When you take the time to extend your right hand to one another in fellowship, you are showing the love of God. In 1 John 1:3, it says, "…that which we have seen and heard we declare to you, that you also may have fellowship with us; and truly our fellowship is with the Father and with His Son Jesus Christ."

Brothers and Sisters in Christ

He who loves his brother abides in the light, and there is no cause for stumbling in him (1 John 2:10).

Mark and I were excited! We were planning on taking another trip to see our son and his family in Europe. There was only one unresolved issue: what to do with Mom while we were away. That always seemed a concern when we wanted to be away for any length of time. I could never leave her alone because of the insulin shots she needed every day. Her medications also had to be monitored since we caught her taking more than the prescribed amount. What a panic I felt the day she took too many heart pills and blood thinners! Mom didn't understand why she couldn't take her own meds without supervision, and she thought I was treating her like a child.

Forgetfulness was not usually a problem for Mom, so there were times when I felt I could leave her for a few hours. If I was going to be gone longer than I'd planned, I'd called to make sure she was fine.

I was learning where the boundaries lay. It got to the point where I could trust her to wait for me to give her the pills. However, if we wanted to be away for several days, we couldn't leave her alone. Our neighbors were always kind and helpful anytime they were needed. They would come and check on her if I asked them to, but I never imposed on them to do more. I was grateful for any help they would give. We also met some wonderful people in our church who offered to come and stay with her. if needed.

We really wanted to go to Germany to see our kids, and so I asked one woman from our church to come and check on Mom and give her the shots and medications she needed. This woman was willing to come by the house every day to do this for us, even if she could not live in with Mom. We decided we were okay with this arrangement, and we were glad that we had encouraged Mom to visit with the church members to get to know them better. Now we were able to go on vacation and be at peace, knowing Mom would be okay. She felt grateful for family and friends who would check in with her during our absence. We were thankful and happy to be part of God's family!

> **Think about this:** The church is God's family, and He has adopted us to be His children. We are to come together for worship, for fellowship with one another, and to be taught from the Word. The church family is there to encourage and lift us up. Praise God! We can be part of His wonderful, supportive family!

The Caregiver's Mission

Brethren, if anyone among you wanders from the truth, and someone turns him back, let him know that he who turns a sinner from the error of his way will save a soul from death and cover a multitude of sins (James 5:19, 20).

Mom was a very difficult woman to deal with at times. She did not seem to have forgiveness for those who had wronged her, especially toward Dad who had been deceased for many years. Despite her hardness when it came to forgiving, Mom had a warm side. Granted, it was hard to see sometimes, but nevertheless it was there. She was very generous to me whenever I needed anything for my house or my family.

Many times I would ask myself the question, "What kind of deeds and actions could I do to show Mom a better way to live?" Mom had a tough life with Dad; she was always saying she had had only a few years in her marriage that were good, even though they were together for forty-seven years! At the beginning, they believed their marriage was sanctioned by God, and they loved each other very much. They enjoyed a few years with Him at the center of their lives. Unfortunately, Dad did not know how to show her the love and attention she required, so he began to lose her. Little by little, she moved away from him as well as from God; she started playing with temptation, which only made things worse. She needed to go back to being right with God.

I am not saying the fault lay only with her. Dad played a big part in what was happening in their lives. If ever they needed God's guidance, it was at the very beginning of their relationship. Unfortunately, the bad choices they made consumed their whole lives. They were never willing to sit down with each other and figure out what to do to turn their lives and their marriage around. As a result, Mom, at the age of 79, was still blaming Dad for everything that had gone wrong in their marriage. She found herself miserable with no peace in her heart. As her caregiver, I had to pray for God to help me find some way to bring her back to Him where she belonged, back to trusting again. It took all of her lifetime to get to this point. What could I do in the short time she had left? I needed God's help, and I didn't even realize how much.

I had the job of not only caring for her physical needs, but her spiritual needs as well. What a tremendous undertaking for a caregiver. Often I would wonder if I was doing everything God wanted me to do for her. I was at a loss and often felt guilty, always thinking of ways to make her last days happier and more peaceful. The only thing I could do was give it to God every day and try to bring the gospel to her.

> **Think about this:** If you have the role of being a caregiver, pray with the one you care for and give them to the Lord. Sometimes you know the story behind their attitudes, and sometimes you don't. Try to bring them to Christ by your attitudes, deeds, and actions. Answer any questions they may have concerning spiritual things the best way you can, knowing that God will take care of the rest. Share how He has helped you to see your sins for what they are and how He forgave you, giving you power to forsake them. Remind them of the prodigal son and how willing his father was to welcome him home—and how much more willing our Heavenly Father is to accept us. Gently try to lead them to Christ through your words and deeds. Only then can you truthfully say, "I have fulfilled my job well and have no regrets."

Living in Harmony

A new commandment I give to you, that you love one another; as I have loved you, that you also love one another. By this all will know that you are My disciples, if you have love for one another (John 13:34, 35).

Living with Mom for a good many years taught me how to be patient, kind, and more loving. I thought I had learned those lessons years before while raising three children, but God had more to teach me. He was still working on my heart, showing me what true love really is. It was unbelievably hard to get used to my mother's ways. Like a marriage, it takes time for two people to adjust. Mom had all kinds of habits that did not sit well with me. One of them was being a shopaholic. While her health didn't allow her to go out shopping, she loved to watch the television shopping channels and buy, buy, buy! Some of the things she wanted to order made no sense, and I felt, at times, that she was wasting the little money she received from her Social Security check.

When I think back on how my attitude toward her was so unloving, I realize that maybe there was a lot about me that Mom had to get used to as well! We had to learn to handle each situation with love and patience. Life would have been much easier for both of us if love and patience had been in our hearts from the beginning. We could have minimized our differences and tried harder to avoid arguments over things that did not matter by concentrating on the things that would bring us together, rather than what divided us.

> **Think about this:** God wants us to be one with one another, having the same love He has for us. As unity is essential in the church, it is also essential in the home. If the members of the church are divided, having their own opinions, doing their own things, and never seeking harmony, how can they be expected to

live with one another in Heaven? As the church works together for the salvation of the world, the home should be working together for the salvation of its family members. Our homes would be more pleasant if we practiced living in harmony. Psalm 133:1 says, "Behold, how good and how pleasant it is for brethren to dwell together in unity!"

Allow God to give you the wisdom that is needed as a caregiver to not agonize over the small stuff as you are caring for His children. Work toward being in harmony with them, showing love, kindness, patience, and understanding.

Becoming Perfect Through Jesus

And the glory which You gave Me I have given them, that they may be one just as We are one: I in them, and You in Me; that they may be made perfect in one, and that the world may know that You have sent Me, and have loved them as You have loved Me (John 17:22, 23).

Being a caregiver enables us to be a witness for God. When I was chosen to care for Mom after her stroke, there was no question what was expected of me. But allowing discouragements to set in also allowed Satan to have his way.

Satan knew how Mom could push my buttons. There were all kinds of things that would irritate me—her shopaholic tendencies and her eating habits were just two of the irritants that we had arguments about. I thought I needed to change her habits if things were ever going to improve in our home, never once thinking that she might have a list of things she wanted to change about me! I thought I was the right one in this relationship. God had so much to teach me about being a caregiver and a loving daughter.

Failure waits at the door when we try to change things ourselves without the help of God

I needed to show more love to Mom, to stop focusing on her faults, and to see her as Jesus saw her. Instead, I tended to focus on what caused a lot of strife between us. I needed to find a way to bring her attention heavenward. She was going through enough without me criticizing her and making things worse. It is amazing how little changes on my part could have brightened both of our days.

Think about this: God wants us to be one with Him. We can only be perfect through Jesus. Failure waits at the door when we try to change things ourselves without the help of God. Begin your day with prayer and invite the Holy Spirit in, asking Him to bring Christ into your heart. When you have Him in there, your thoughts will not be on yourself, but on Him. You will be more cheerful and will help make everyone around you happy. Thank God for the gift He has given you, the gift of being a caregiver, no matter how difficult some days will surely be. Through this gift you can speak the truth in love and grow in Christ. Ephesians 4:15, 16 says, "…but, speaking the truth in love, may grow up in all things into Him who is the head—Christ—from whom the whole body, joined and knit together by what every joint supplies, according to the effective working by which every part does its share, causes growth of the body for the edifying of itself in love."

How can you have love like Jesus did and be perfect through Him? This may seem to be impossible, but start at the cross and see what Jesus did. You will then understand what He said in John 15:5, "I am the vine, you are the branches. He who abides in Me, and I in him, bears much fruit; for without Me you can do nothing." The cross shows that Jesus loves everyone. When He lives in your heart, you will seek unity with all those around you.

Dealing with Indecision

Have I not commanded you? Be strong and of good courage; do not be afraid, nor be dismayed, for the Lord your God is with you wherever you go
(Joshua 1:9).

I took care of Mom for seven years. Toward the end of those years, she told me that, if anything ever happened to her, she did not want us to bring her back to life. She had completed all the proper "Do Not Resuscitate" (DNR) paperwork; she was tired and ready to go. I did not want to hear that because I loved her, and I could not picture a time without her. We had our ups and downs during the course of time, but we still loved each other. However, the time did come when we had to say goodbye. During that time, I found myself having to make a very tough decision—probably the hardest decision of my life.

It started when we returned from a wonderful weekend with my son and his wife. Mom was in good hands with people from the church, and our neighbors checked in on her as well. I called Mom regularly while we were away to make sure everything was alright. We got back late Sunday night to find Mom in great spirits. We talked for a while, but we were tired after that long trip and were ready for bed, and so we said our goodnights.

The next morning, I awoke still feeling tired. I was doing some things in my room when I saw Mom coming down the hall holding her stomach. She stopped by my door and explained to me that she was not feeling very well. She did not know what was wrong with her. All of a sudden she felt very nauseated and started vomiting. She never wanted me to call the doctor, so I just helped her into bed and tried to take care of her the best I could. It looked to me as if she had a stomach virus. I thought that all she needed was a lot of rest and liquids to get better. But she grew progressively worse. By nightfall, I was relieved when she finally fell asleep, which enabled me to get some rest, too.

When I woke up the next morning and went to check on her, I immediately knew something was seriously wrong. The upper part of her body was very hot, and the lower part of her body was cold. Her stomach was the size of a small baseball. She was not a very big woman, so I could really see the bulge near her stomach. I told her that there must be another problem, and that I was going to call the ambulance. The paramedics came immediately and, with all the excitement that was going on, I forgot to give them her DNR paperwork. As they tried to treat her, she died three times in our kitchen, but the paramedics kept bringing her back. She finally made it to the hospital where they ran a lot of tests. They told her she had a perforated bowel and that she was not going to survive. She became septic very quickly with the infection spreading throughout her bloodstream, and they did not think surgery would help the situation.

I called all four of her other children and told them what was happening. I put the phone on speaker so each one could say something to her. It was wonderful to see her eyes light up as she was listening to each of her children talking to her. She could not talk back because of the tubes down her throat, but she could listen with her ears, and those were the most touching goodbyes I have ever witnessed.

I knew Mom was going to die no matter what, but the decision that I had to make was devastating for me. I could see the fear in her eyes. She always said she wanted me to let her go when it was that time, but the look that she had as she really faced death was telling me something different. Oh, the tough decision I had to make that night. I asked the nurse how long we would have to wait for her to breathe her last if we decided to remove the tubes, and the nurse said only five minutes. I knew in my heart that I had to make the right decision—the decision she had said she wanted—and that was to let her go. I told the nurses to please take out the tubes. I will never forget that last five minutes of her life. Mark and I were at her bedside, praying, holding her hands, and just being there for her. What a time of indecision that had been. I just had to know the facts and then, know what Mom had always said to me while we were together concerning her health, and then I could go from there.

Think about this: There may be times in your life when you will have to deal with uncertainty, especially if you are a caregiver. You may have to make some pretty tough decisions, uncertain as to whether or not you are making the right ones. It will never be easy, but you have the assurance that you are not alone. God is there to help and guide you through it all. Remember Joshua 1:9, this section's Scripture verse, and know that He is with you all the time.

God's Watch Care over His Children
A Beautiful Story of God's Leading

Trust in the Lord with all your heart, and lean not on your own understanding; in all your ways acknowledge Him, and He shall direct your paths (Prov. 3:5, 6).

After Mom's passing, we were able to open our home once a week to entertain people. While mom was with us, she made it perfectly clear that too many visitors made her nervous. She did not mind a few, but to open our home every week was a little too much for her. I always tried to abide by her wishes to make her happy. Now that she was no longer with us, we could open our home after church to anyone who wanted to come.

Our church was located in colonial Williamsburg, Virginia, a beautiful tourist town with lots of wonderful places to visit. People from all over the world came to see the attractions. Our church enjoyed a lot of visitors, sometimes making up half of the congregation. My husband, Mark, and I had a burden to open our home to welcome these wonderful people after church, so they do not have to go back to their hotels or campers and spend God's day by themselves. We wanted them to feel welcomed and blessed, so we invited them to our home.

One beautiful spring day, we prepared for many visitors after church. But God had a surprise for us this day. At church, we met a lot of visitors and we invited all of them—as well as some church members—to share a meal with us. Quite a few accepted our invitation. A few of the visitors were from Puerto Rico, and some came from Maryland. We were so excited that we could feed them and get to know them better. The day went well, and, before they left, I had them sign our personal guest book, so I could send them a thank-you card for coming to visit us. I also gave them my business card, so they would not forget us either.

That evening after everyone had left, we settled down to relax a little before retiring for the night. I had already gone to bed when the phone rang. I did not recognize the caller's number, but I answered anyway. The voice on the other end was unfamiliar, but I soon realized that it was one of the visitors from Puerto Rico. I sensed that something was wrong. The woman told us that they were stranded and had no vehicle. Apparently, they had checked out of their accommodations before church started, thinking they would travel on, but a misunderstanding had left them without a place to stay or a means of transportation. It was the busy tourist season, and most of the hotels were full.

I told my husband what happened, and we quickly dressed and drove to the hotel where the women were stranded. When we arrived, we found them sitting in the front of the hotel. We threw our arms around them and told them everything was going to be okay. We assured them that they were welcome in our home and could stay with us until they would return home the following week. That turned out to be the most wonderful experience for Mark and me. They rented a car and were able to continue their visit to our lovely region. It was a beautiful experience, and I was very thankful that I had given them my business card. We felt that God had introduced us to part of His wonderful family that week, the lovely family of God!

Think about this: God does watch over His children; and, if they need help, He will send just the right people to cross their path. He knows who will respond to their needs. You can be one of those caregivers God can use. Always be ready without hesitation to be on call. You will never know what a wonderful blessing you could receive unless you step out of your comfort zone, and let God lead. The blessing will not only be on you, but on the lives you are touching. How different this all might have turned out for our Puerto Rican friends if they had not accepted our invitation to a meal and fellowship that afternoon. We must treat each other with love and respect. Remember that golden rule, to treat others as you would have them treat you, and trust in the Lord to direct you in all of your paths.

Blessing Others

Let them do good, that they be rich in good works, ready to give, willing to share, storing up for themselves a good foundation for the time to come, that they may lay hold on eternal life (1 Tim. 6:18, 19).

One warm summer day, I was outdoors raking in my yard when I glanced over to my neighbor's house. Gary and Michaela were caring people who had helped us when we first moved into our home. They were always there when we needed them. They would pick up our mail, if needed. When Mom was still with us, they would check on her if we had to leave for a while. Oftentimes the feeling of being blessed was overwhelming. There were Christian neighbors all around us. When God chose this place, He not only thought to give us an appropriate dwelling to reside in, but He knew we would need kind neighbors who would be helpful, especially with taking care of Mom while she was alive. It surely gave me peace of mind and a thankful heart!

As I was looking at Michaela's home, I became aware that her car had not moved out of the driveway in a while, which was unusual because she had a job. I had also seen a strange vehicle coming to her home on more than one occasion. A sudden thought came to me to call her when I was finished raking. But as I raked, the thought grew stronger to call right away and not wait. As I was about to put down my rake her husband drove in. When he got out of the car, I called to him and asked how everything was. He responded with just an, "Okay," but that answer did not satisfy me. Pursuing it further, I told him about my impression to call Michaela to see if there was anything wrong. He then explained that she had broken her leg the week before. I immediately offered my services, cleaning and cooking for them that summer. They had always been such a blessing to us, and now God was giving me the opportunity to be a blessing to them. They greatly appreciated my efforts, and I felt richly rewarded. Helping this family who had helped us brought me such happiness.

Think about this: Doing for others can bring a feeling of great satisfaction and joy because you know you are pleasing Jesus. Matthew 25:40 says, "And the King will answer and say to them, 'Assuredly, I say to you, inasmuch as you did it to one of the least of these My brethren, you did it to Me.'" As you give to Jesus, you will be rewarded greatly for your efforts, and everything you do will contribute to your well-being. Develop love and generous attributes like Jesus, and you will live a life of gratitude and unselfishness, becoming a faithful steward, spreading the gospel to the world by your actions.

Sharing the Good News—Jesus Is Coming Again!

And behold, I am coming quickly, and My reward is with Me, to give to every one according to his work (Rev. 22:12).

Graduation Day! It was going to be one of the best days of my life. I had worked hard for this because, unlike the average high-school graduate, I was forty years old! As children, my parents never encouraged us to finish school. The decision to quit, at the age of sixteen to help out with the finances at home, was an easy one to make. However, I made myself a promise to go back and finish my education someday.

Years later, the day came when the opportunity presented itself. My last child was in school, so this was the perfect time for me to return to my studies. I enrolled in an adult education program to earn not just a GED, but a real high-school diploma. This was not going to be easy though, because I was also working to help pay our boys' school tuition. But I was determined, and so, with the support of my husband, I began.

When my first class began, I was struck with terror! I was convinced that I was not smart enough to do this. Mark was a great encouragement to me and even attended some of the classes with me. The next four years were hard. God and Mark helped me make it, inch by inch, to the finish line. Graduation night finally arrived, and having my family and church members there to celebrate the occasion really boosted my morale! When I walked down the aisle to get my diploma that I had worked so hard for and heard the shouts of approval from everyone, I felt like a winner! I had reached the finish line and accomplished my goal.

Think about this: Jesus is coming again! This knowledge provides such hope for Christians everywhere! Everything we do now on earth should point to Jesus's coming to take us home.

That will be our ultimate graduation day! We are to be a witness to everyone around us that we have this hope; that there is something better than what this world has to offer. Every day you are working for Christ, while you long for that wonderful day when He will come. Share the good news of the gospel with everyone you meet.

As workers for the Lord, you have the opportunity to help people get ready to be with Jesus. Some are nearing death and may have never heard the good news of Jesus coming back to take them home. While the ones you care for are still alive, continue to give them the hope of something better than what they know now. Work with a happy heart. Take the time to bring those precious souls you are caring for to Jesus, so they too can have the blessed hope and be able to say in that day: "Behold, this is our God; we have waited for Him, and He will save us. This is the Lord; we have waited for Him; we will be glad and rejoice in His salvation" (Isa. 25:9). May we all be there on that graduation day and hear those shouts of approval from our heavenly angels! Praise God!

The Death Sentence

And the Lord God commanded the man, saying, "Of every tree of the garden you may freely eat; but of the tree of the knowledge of good and evil you shall not eat, for in the day that you eat of it you shall surely die" (Gen. 2:16, 17).

The Tree of the Knowledge of Good and Evil was placed in the Garden of Eden as a test given by God to see if humankind loved God enough to obey Him. God told Adam and Eve that they could have everything in the garden except for the fruit of that one forbidden tree. God, in His merciful way, clearly explained to them the consequences of disobeying this order. Satan was not allowed to pursue Adam and Eve with temptations. The only place he could have access to them was at this one tree. Should they attempt to investigate this forbidden tree, the couple would be exposed to Satan's wiles.

Eve spent her time with Adam, tending the beautiful garden that God had given to them. They were the first caregivers, in charge of caring for each other and the garden that God had given them as their home. The angels had warned Eve to beware of separating herself from Adam, because she would be in greater danger of temptation if she were alone. One day, she was so involved in her tasks that she unconsciously wandered away from Adam. When she realized she was by herself, she felt the danger, but dismissed her fears. She decided she had enough wisdom and strength to discern evil and to withstand it if she had to.

Not thinking of the angels' caution, she soon found herself gazing with admiration at the forbidden tree. The fruit was very beautiful, and she could not help wondering why God withheld it from them. Satan was watching her, and he seized this opportunity to beguile her by disguising himself as a talking serpent. As she was standing there, she suddenly heard a voice speaking to her.

We all know the results of that conversation. Satan, speaking through the serpent, told Eve lies. He explained how she could not possibly die by eating from that beautiful tree. He told lies about God, causing her to question God's command not to touch the fruit. Satan continued on this evil track until Eve took and ate the fruit. Excitement mounted in her when nothing bad seemed to be happening, so she took some of the fruit to her husband, Adam. He knew better than to touch that fruit, but he complied, willing to share the consequences because of his great love for her.

Think about this: Since that fateful day, this world has been dying. We see it all around us as we watch our loved ones die, and we know that we ourselves will suffer the same fate someday. Our bodies are not immortal. Only God is immortal. In 1 Timothy 6:16, speaking of God, it says, "Who alone has immortality, dwelling in unapproachable light, whom no man has seen or can see, to whom be honor and everlasting power." James 4:14 says, "Whereas you do not know what will happen tomorrow. For what is your life? It is even a vapor that appears for a little time and then vanishes away."

What is death? Ecclesiastes 9:5, 6 says, "For the living know that they will die; but the dead know nothing, and they have no more reward, for the memory of them is forgotten. Also their love, their hatred, and their envy have now perished; never more will they have a share in anything done under the sun."

Is the grave the only thing we have to look forward to? Did God give Adam and Eve no hope? As you are caring for one another, whether you are a parent, a teacher, or some other kind of caregiver, is there anything you can say to encourage others? Study God's word together and find out just what He has to offer us. Let us look past the sentence of death, and have the hope that only He can give us.

Hope after Death

Behold, I tell you a mystery: We shall not all sleep, but we shall all be changed—in a moment, in the twinkling of an eye, at the last trumpet. For the trumpet will sound, and the dead will be raised incorruptible, and we shall be changed. For this corruptible must put on incorruption, and this mortal must put on immortality (1 Cor. 15:51–53).

As we continue to read the Bible, we find out that there is more for us than the death sentence following that first disobedience in the Garden of Eden. Romans 6:23 says, "For the wages of sin is death, but the gift of God is eternal life in Christ Jesus our Lord." This is a Scripture that is full of hope! Death does not have to be our final destination. In 1 Corinthians 15:22, it says, "For as in Adam all die, even so in Christ all shall be made alive." God has devised a plan to save us. The Son of God was willing to give His life in our place, so we could have a second chance!

Before Mom passed away, I always tried to encourage her by telling her about the second chance God was offering her. I talked about death being just a sleep and how we will awaken from death, as if in a moment, to see the lovely face of Jesus if we die holding onto God's promise of eternal life through Jesus. The passing of time is not felt when we go to sleep at night and awaken in the morning. Death is similar. As Mom was breathing her last breath, with me sitting by her bedside holding her hand, I said, "See you in the morning Mom, I love you."

> *The Bible tells us of a resurrection morning. It encourages us to know that we can enjoy a future life beyond death and anything this old world has to offer*

The Bible tells us of a resurrection morning. It encourages us to know that we can enjoy a future life beyond death and anything this old world has to offer. We know that, if it were not for Christ's resurrection, there would not be any hope for eternal life for us. There would be no reason to preach the good news of the gospel.

In 1 Corinthians 15:14, it says, "And if Christ be not risen, then our preaching is vain, and your faith is also vain" (KJV). But we do have the hope of a resurrection because of what Jesus did for us. In John 5:28, 29, it says, "Do not marvel at this; for the hour is coming in which all who are in the graves will hear His voice and come forth—those who have done good, to the resurrection of life, and those who have done evil, to the resurrection of condemnation."

> **Think about this:** There is hope for humanity! In 2 Timothy 1:10, it tells us that this eternal hope is in "…our Savior Jesus Christ, who has abolished death and brought life and immortality to light through the gospel." By sharing this good news, we can give hope to all. The ones you lovingly care for no longer have to wonder what the future holds. Bring them the hope they need, so that, when they breathe their last, there will be no fear, only an anticipation of being part of the resurrection and of finally seeing the face of their sweet Jesus.

Getting a People Ready

*But the heavens and the earth which now preserved by the
same word, are reserved for fire until the day of judgment
and perdition of ungodly men* (2 Peter 3:7).

Resisting God's love is never a good thing. He only has our best interest in mind, and He wants us to be saved by Him and live with Him in His kingdom. Everything He tells us to do is because He loves us. This is His only motive, and He knows it will make us happier in the end. It is the same way when we are caring for another person. Sometimes they can be stubborn and not want to hear what we have to say. I found this was the case many times while I was taking care of Mom.

When I first started to care for her, she did not want to eat a healthy diet, and I felt she was making herself sick. She resisted what I had to say. If I had insisted on doing things my way rather than letting God deal with it, our relationship would have suffered. Then we had another issue that made us both miserable. She had cataracts in both eyes. Time and time again, my attempts to encourage her to get them removed only brought strife between us. She did not realize I only wanted her to see well, so that she could have a more fulfilling life. My motive for wanting to help her was always love, but my methods were imperfect. And every time I tried to reach out to her, she resisted. It is the same thing that we do to God. He only wants to help us, but sometimes we resist Him.

The day Mom died reminded me of how fast life can be taken away. She had health complications, and those took her life in just a few days. During those last moments of her life, as I was sitting in the hospital with her, she was awake and alert. However, her breathing was very shallow. I remember praying for God to take her quickly, to stop the suffering, and within minutes she was gone. It brought to my mind the reality that death is final. There is no coming back to this old life. If we have not made things right with God at the end, we will not get a second chance. What a convicting thought! We have to ask the question now: Where do we want to spend eternity? I want to be among the saints when Jesus comes back the second time. I pray that is your goal, too.

Think about this: God has given all the caregivers of this world a wonderful work to do. If you happen to be blessed with this ministry, do not let an opportunity pass by without telling the ones you care for what they need to know, so they can get ready for heaven.

God will create all things new someday, and sin will never rear its ugly head again. The righteous will have learned how fair God is, and what sin really does. They have no desire to ever sin again.

In 2 Peter 3:11, 12, it says, "Therefore, since all these things will be dissolved, what manner of persons ought you to be in holy conduct and godliness, looking for and hastening the coming of the day of God, because of which the heavens will be dissolved, being on fire, and the elements will melt with fervent heat?" As a caregiver and one who is looking forward to this New Earth, make every effort to be found without spot and to be at peace with Christ. Your heart will then be full of love and a longing to encourage the ones you are caring for.

A New Life

Now I saw a new heaven and a new earth, for the first heaven and the first earth had passed away. Also there was no more sea....And God will wipe away every tear from their eyes; there shall be no more death, nor sorrow, nor crying. There shall be no more pain, for the former things have passed away (Rev. 21:1–4).

No more sickness, death, or dying? What a concept! Sickness and death is all we know in this old world. It is all around, and it can strike us or our loved ones at any moment. I watched Dad die of lung disease, lingering on for years until he finally died. Mom died in just a few hours, but she was not well for years. Death knows no age limit. Little babies and children die from illness or accident. My brother Dennis and his wife had a beautiful set of twins. One of them was born with a disease. She had very painful bumps all over her tiny body. This illness did not allow her to grow. It was terrible to watch the suffering this little one had to endure. She died at the age of seven months, weighing only six pounds. When we see all of this going on around us, we are comforted to know that Jesus is coming back to make all things new.

> **Think about this:** Scripture tells us that in the New Earth everything will be made new. Animals will be tame, and we will not fear them. Isaiah 65:25 says, "The wolf and the lamb shall feed together, the lion shall eat straw like the ox, and dust shall be the serpent's food. They shall not hurt or destroy in all My holy mountain, says the Lord." This is going to be a real world that we shall hear, see, smell, taste, and fully experience if we have chosen Christ as our Savior. In 2 Peter 3:13, it says, "Nevertheless we, according to His promise, look for new heavens and a new earth in which righteousness dwells."

What a place God has prepared for us! John says He is preparing a place with wonderful homes for us to live in, real homes (John 14:1–3).[14] In that place, we will be with Jesus and worship Him forever. Jesus wants us to share this good news with everyone we meet, including the sick and dying, giving them hope for a future with God and a home for eternity to look forward to.

Inheriting the Earth and Living Forever!

They shall build houses and inhabit them; they shall plant vineyards and eat their fruit. They shall not build and another inhabit; they shall not plant and another eat; For as the days of a tree, so shall be the days of My people, and My elect shall long enjoy the work of their hands
(Isa. 65:21, 22).

The New Earth! Oh, how happy we will be living there! We will constantly enjoy our beautiful new homes that have been prepared for us. Everything about that place will be exciting! When hungry, all we will have to do is pick the wonderful fruit from the trees that God has created. But this isn't all there is to do while living on the New Earth! We will not only have homes in the city, but we will build our own homes in the country! Picture the rolling hills, beautiful flowers, and peaceful lakes everywhere. Our hands will not be idle, for they will be planting gardens, and the crops that come up will be more delicious than we can ever imagine. Never have we tasted such produce! God himself gave us the urge to create way back in the Garden of Eden. How wonderful it will be to use our minds and hands in a constructive way.

Some of the same family and friends we now know will be there. Just as Mary and Jesus's disciples recognized their Lord after His resurrection, we will also recognize our loved ones. The apostle John tells us that Mary recognized her Lord's voice after He had risen from the dead (John 20:11–16).[15] The disciple Luke tells us that Jesus's disciples recognized Him by how He broke bread with them. (Luke 24:30, 31, 35).[16] The disciples recognized Jesus when He appeared to them in the upper room. He was not a spirit, but real flesh and blood, and we will be the same.

When we think about all of the things God is planning to give us in the future, it helps us to be steadfast during the trials we endure here on earth. Christ Himself said in Matthew 5:12, "Rejoice and be exceedingly glad, for great is your reward in heaven, for so they persecuted the prophets who were before you." Looking forward to this reward gives us the strength we need to fight against temptation. Moses looked forward to this reward. Hebrews 11:24–26 says, "By faith Moses, when he became of age, refused to be called the son of Pharaoh's daughter, choosing rather to suffer affliction with the people of God than to enjoy the passing pleasures of sin, esteeming the reproach of Christ greater riches than the treasures in Egypt; for he looked to the reward."

> **Think about this:** We will have our reward in Heaven and on the New Earth. On this old earth we know that all good things must end, but, on the New Earth, it will never end. Sin and sinners will be no more, and the great controversy between good and evil will finally be over. What a wonderful opportunity you have as a caregiver to proclaim the good news that Jesus is coming back someday to take us home, "…and so shall we ever be with the Lord" (1 Thess. 4:17, KJV). We will never remember this old life of pain and suffering again. Isaiah 65:17 says, "For behold, I create new heavens and a new earth; and the former shall not be remembered or come to mind." Praise God! I want to be part of it all, don't you? Let us work hard to bring people to Jesus before it is too late.

God bless you as you minister in His name,

Nancy

Scriptural Index
NKJV

1. **John 3:23**
   Now John also was baptizing in Aenon near Salim, because there was much water there. And they came and were baptized.

2. **Romans 6:3, 4**
   Or do you not know that as many of us as were baptized into Christ Jesus were baptized into His death? Therefore we were buried with Him through baptism into death, that just as Christ was raised from the dead by the glory of the Father, even so we also should walk in newness of life.

3. **Hebrews 4:16**
   Let us therefore come boldly to the throne of grace, that we may obtain mercy and find grace to help in time of need.

4. **Psalm 24:1**
   The earth is the Lord's, and all its fullness, the world and those who dwell therein.

5. **Matthew 25:24, 26---30**
   "Then he who had received one talent came and said, '…I was afraid, and went and hid your talent in the ground….'But his lord answered and said to him, 'You wicked and lazy servant, you knew that I reap where I have not sown, and gather where I have not scattered seed. So you ought to have deposited my money with the bankers, and at my coming I would have received back my own with interest. So take the talent from him, and give it to him who has ten talents. For to everyone who has, more will be given, and he will have abundance; but from him who does not have, even what he has will be taken away.

And cast the unprofitable servant into the outer darkness. There will be weeping and gnashing of teeth.'"

6. **John 13:3–10**
Jesus, knowing that the Father had given all things into His hands, and that He had come from God and was going to God, rose from supper and laid aside His garments, took a towel and girded Himself. After that, He poured water into a basin and began to wash the disciples' feet, and to wipe them with the towel with which he was girded. Then He came to Simon Peter. And Peter said to Him, "Lord, are You washing my feet?" Jesus answered and said to him, "What I am doing you do not understand now, but you will know after this." Peter said to Him, "You shall never wash my feet!" Jesus answered him, "If I do not wash you, you have no part with Me." Simon Peter said to Him, "Lord, not my feet only, but also my hands and my head!" Jesus said to him, "He who is bathed needs only to wash his feet, but is completely clean; and you are clean, but not all of you."

7. **Matthew 20:28**
"…Just as the Son of Man did not come to be served, but to serve, and to give His life a ransom for many."

8. **John 13:1**
Now before the Feast of the Passover, when Jesus knew that His hour had come that He should depart from this world to the Father, having loved His own who were in the world, He loved them to the end.

9. **Galatians 5:22, 23**
But the fruit of the Spirit is love, joy, peace, longsuffering, kindness, goodness, faithfulness, gentleness, self-control. Against such there is no law.

10. **John 16:7**
Nevertheless I tell you the truth. It is to your advantage that I go away; for if I do not go away, the Helper will not come to you; but if I depart, I will send Him to you.

11. **Psalm 139:14**
I will praise You, for I am fearfully and wonderfully made; Marvelous are Your works, and that my soul knows very well.

12. **Zechariah 3:1–4**

    Then he showed me Joshua the high priest standing before the Angel of the Lord, and Satan standing at his right hand to oppose him. And the Lord said to Satan, "The Lord rebuke you, Satan! The Lord who has chosen Jerusalem rebuke you! Is this not a brand plucked from the fire?" Now Joshua was clothed with filthy garments, and was standing before the Angel. Then He answered and spoke to those who stood before Him, saying, "Take away the filthy garments from him." And to him He said, "See, I have removed your iniquity from you, and I will clothe you with rich robes."

13. **Romans 8:28**

    And we know that all things work together for good to those who love God, to those who are the called according to His purpose.

14. **John 14:1–3**

    "Let not your heart be troubled; you believe in God, believe also in Me. In My Father's house are many mansions; if it were not so, I would have told you. I go to prepare a place for you. And if I go and prepare a place for you, I will come again and receive you to Myself; that where I am, there you may be also."

15. **John 20:11–16**

    But Mary stood outside by the tomb weeping, and as she wept she stooped down and looked into the tomb. And she saw two angels in white sitting, one at the head and the other at the feet, where the body of Jesus had lain. Then they said to her, "Woman, why are you weeping?" She said to them, "Because they have taken away my Lord, and I do not know where they have laid Him." Now when she had said this, she turned around and saw Jesus standing there, and did not know that it was Jesus. Jesus said to her, "Woman, why are you weeping? Whom are you seeking?" She, supposing Him to be the gardener, said to Him, "Sir, if You have carried Him away, tell me where You have laid Him, and I will take Him away." Jesus said to her, "Mary!" She turned and said to Him, "Rabboni!" (which is to say, Teacher).

16. **Luke 24:30, 31, 35**

    Now it came to pass, as He sat at the table with them, that He took bread, blessed and broke it, and gave it to them. Then their eyes were opened and they knew Him; and He vanished from their sight .... And they told about the things that had happened on the road, and how He was known to them in the breaking of bread.

References

Other books written by the Author

Journey to a Better Land

Journey to a Better Land: Inspirational Gems (Three-Volume Audio Book)

God's Power Revealed Through Prayer

About the Author

Nancy Berthiaume LaPierre lives in Newport News, Virginia, with her husband, Mark. She decided to share what she learned as a caregiver, with the prayer that her experiences would be an encouragement to others. Throughout her life she has taken care of many precious souls who were in need—young and old. Most recently she cared for her mom until her passing. Those seven years proved to be not only a time of challenge, but also a time of joy.

It is her wish that these writings will help caregivers everywhere turn to God when they need Him. She hopes all caregivers will share with everyone they meet the bright future that awaits those who give their hearts to Jesus.

TEACH Services, Inc.
P U B L I S H I N G

We invite you to view the complete
selection of titles we publish at:
www.TEACHServices.com

We encourage you to write us
with your thoughts about this,
or any other book we publish at:
info@TEACHServices.com

TEACH Services' titles may be purchased in
bulk quantities for educational, fund-raising,
business, or promotional use.
bulksales@TEACHServices.com

Finally, if you are interested in seeing
your own book in print, please contact us at:
publishing@TEACHServices.com

We are happy to review your manuscript at no charge.

www.ingramcontent.com/pod-product-compliance
Lightning Source LLC
Chambersburg PA
CBHW020358170426
43200CB00005B/217